Temple

The Science Behind the Spirituality of Health

Marcia Enos

For my family...

Table of Contents

Introduction

We are incredibly lucky to be alive today. We are beginning to understand many things that were considered miracles or magic by past generations. Teleportation of protons across 88 miles is a reality. Scientists can transport protons instantaneously across the world or rather, transport the information, which makes the proton a specific proton. They do it using crystals and lasers. Scientists can cloak something and make it seem invisible using Plexiglas materials and copper rings. We can float in the air. Super conductors can be made using ceramics and liquid nitrogen to create what seems to be an anti-gravity train. The train floats above its track when an electrical pulse is applied to the track. We can turn on a computer, connect to invisible information waves called a wireless network, and learn about how our universe is constructed. New information is being added faster and faster, and this includes understanding how the tiny particles in our bodies are put together.

Today, we can study the elegance of the human body without invading it with scalpels. We are lucky enough to live in a time when we can receive any number of different scans that employ the different frequencies of the electromagnetic field to tell us about the inner workings of our bodies. We are swimming in an alphabet soup of imaging and measuring. MRI, CT, PET, EEG, EKG, Sonograms, and X-rays all help us to check on the functional and structural integrity of our bodies. These tests applied together with the emerging study of biophysics, a synthesis of the principles of physics, computer modeling, mathematical analysis, and biological systems enable us to understand just how beautifully our body temples commingle with the universe.

Modern scientists measure the currents that run through our nerves, how our environment sends messages to our brains, and how our brains redirect those currents of energy to move, speak and perceive. They can measure the chemical messengers that tell us to be hungry, happy or fearful, and give us new insights about how we can manage our bodies for the best health ever. Unfortunately, all of these informative scans, tests, and imaging techniques cost a small fortune. At a time when good healthcare is hard to afford and even harder to receive in a timely fashion, it becomes critically important to learn how to gain and maintain our health. It seems today's healthcare is a series of medications that mask some symptoms while causing others that are sometimes worse. I watch as friends that are too young for Medicare literally worry themselves sick over the financial burden of healthcare. Others have lost their homes to pay for hospital care and prescriptions that didn't really heal them. I wonder if the Bible gives us a better way?

What does the Bible say about taking care of the body? I know about the old testament rules regarding meat and dairy, and other foods, but what about all the other things that we are guided to do like praying, meditating, giving thanks, trusting, doing good to others, singing and such? What does the new research on these subjects show us? Is the Bible right? What life instructions are contained in the Bible? Are they valuable in shaping our health? And if they are effective, why do they work? Well, the Bible says, "seek and you shall find," so that is what I set out to do.

I am so glad that you are interested in the commonalities between God and science. The subject is something that I have been interested in for years. I love all the sciences; chemistry, physics, ecology, biology, anatomy, physiology, botany, geology, and astronomy, though stopping at first year calculus holds me back from the formal study of physics. I have no formal religious training and am far from perfect. When I was young, I was brought to church on a rickety old school bus. The bus was operated by a new church, where dedicated, loving individuals walked door to door every Saturday to farm the neighborhood for new children to recruit. On Sunday mornings, these same individuals would pick up children and drive them to and from Sunday school. The lessons that I learned were simple; God loves you and so do these people. Coming from a home where my two alcoholic parents were more than happy to get rid of my two siblings and myself, I thrived attending there; and that church, with its youth group, became my family for a little while.

As I grew up, I began to question the validity of the Bible and the men that taught it. My harsh home life gave me no reason to trust. So, questioning is a large part of my personality. Is there a God? If so, how does this Spirit entity interact with my life? I read the Bible completely twice on my own but stopped attending church. I read it for its history and also paying close attention to the red ink, the words of Jesus. That is the extent of my Biblical training: Sunday school and self-study. Knowing the history of the Bible, it is easy to question if the Bible is a Divine tool of instruction, or just a method used by kings and churches to control people. How should the Bible be read? Is it literal or always an interpretation of stories? Why stories? Can its stories, analogies, and metaphors really help me in my life?

Having been a good student in Sunday school, I remember many of the verses that I memorized and the stories that I enjoyed as a child. I remember that the Bible told us we were "Temples of the Holy Spirit", but what does it mean to be a temple? What does that title or phrase tell us about ourselves?

What is the great "I Am" anyway? God is supposed to be everywhere at once and never ending. What does science have to say about it?

All authors want to start their books off with a big bang. The Big Bang we will consider in this book isn't the one taught in schools. It isn't the one that asks us to believe a chaotic explosion ended with a perfectly designed universe. Advances in physics allow us to look inside our universe and its source. Where did the universe come from and what has the universe got to do with God or us? Scientists' ability to trace, measure, and calculate smaller and smaller particles of energy enables them to discover new insights into how the universe interrelates with our bodies, within our bodies, and with our environment. I wanted to examine the Bible's instructions simultaneously with these new insights to gain a new perspective on how we are told to live and why.

Being an Environmental scientist, I wondered what our role in the environment we call earth is. How should we interact with the plants, animals and environment around us? I wanted to know what the Bible tells us about how we should care for the world and the others that we share it with. We live in a world filled with toxic chemicals and pay for clean water. Is this what God had in mind for us when we were given rule over the earth? Epigenetics, the branch of genetics that studies the changeable or plastic controls over our DNA, shows us that our environment has as much or in some cases, a much larger influence over the state of our bodies than our genes. Are crowded feedlots, polluted rivers and lakes, and toxic wastes spewing into the air and in our waters what God expected from us? How do toxins affect our health? Environmental toxins can overwhelm our livers, our Guts, and the microorganisms that live inside of us to help keep us healthy. We have more tiny bacteria living in our digestive tract than cells making up our bodies. How can we take care of our temples and the environment to stay healthier?

What should we eat to be healthy? What does the Bible tells us about over-eating? Yes, there are instructions about over-eating. The Bible contains warnings concerning the outcome if one does over-eat and it has a path to become free from any addiction including food cravings. Clinical double-blind studies have shown that the methods included in the Bible to overcome our addictions are truly effective and benefit our bodies in ways that extend our lives.

Using fluorescent dyes, imaging and clinical evidence to prove what we eat is important, scientists also show us that when and how we eat is important. "To everything there is a season" is true regarding our bodies. When we eat and sleep alters our hormone cycles. The cycles of hormones and their interactions with ingested foods affect our moods, our energy levels, our sleep patterns, and our immunity. Fat cells act like they are part of the endocrine system. They can make, release and alter hormones in our bodies. They play an essential role in whether or not we have a healthy immune system. They can cause increased inflammation. Excess fat influences whether we are prone to cancers and influences the function of our brains as well. The timing of our eating, sleeping and playing interrelate to influence our metabolisms.

What does the Bible say about staying happy as well as healthy? What does science say about those directions? In Genesis, we are told that God gave us herbs. The science of phytochemistry tells us how herbs and plants that heal and maintain our physical and mental health work by isolating their active constituents. Did you know that Valproic Acid, which is extracted from Valerian Root, is one of the main ingredients in many prescription anti-anxiety medications? We have all heard of antioxidants and free radicals but did you know that the Good Samaritan used the powerful antioxidants and anti-microbials in olive oil to help save the beaten man? Happiness and health are best maintained by taking a whole person approach to them. The Bible does just that. Neuroanatomy and epigenetics explain the reasons why social and personal growth is necessary to maintain and encourage healthy bodies and minds.

The directions that the Bible gave us can be held up to the light and analyzed for literal efficacy. Today, we can ask why and find the answers. This book is for the spiritual person that questions everything, including anything I write. It's more than OK to understand science and the incredible way that it can be used to prove the merit behind the Bible's simple directions on how to live. My purpose is not to prove the existence of God or the divineness of the Bible, but merely to look at the Bible both literally and figuratively, holding some of its directions about our bodies and our minds up to the light of science today.

When I began writing and researching, this book was about the herbs in the Bible. But, this book went its own way. It was as though all my studies and all of my interests had congregated into this volume. You can postulate that I looked for scientific evidence to prove the verses in the Bible, a proverbial cherry picker. This is true! Again I say, "Seek and ye shall find." It doesn't make the scientific evidence less provoking. I hope that you will search the facts out for yourself and continue to look for other studies and data. Wonderfully, science is evolving all of the time.

Parables and the Universe

Each of us experience life from our own center point, ourselves. The stories found in the Bible allow each of us to interpret their meanings. The stories are common to all types of Christian churches including Catholic, Fundamentalist and Charismatic alike. Some of the stories, such as the flood, are found in almost every culture. Maybe, the fact that these lessons are found across the world is what was meant in Revelation 5 verse 9, "from every tribe, and language and people and nation will be saved".

We learn as children the stories about: the creation, the garden, the flood, and the Good Samaritan, just to name a few. Many of us grew up learning the morals of each story found in the Old and New Testaments, but what if there is more to the stories than just moral values? What if the stories have more literal lessons to teach? Physics and epigenetics have created new ground from which we can examine the stories in more literal terms. Many books have been written expounding on the similarities of quantum physics and eastern philosophies but not much has been written that compares our traditional Christian parables or stories to modern sciences. The deeper I dove into the comparisons, the more I found. I am still finding them in journals on the Internet that can be accessed on Pubmed, a National Institutes of Health website. I hope that you can find the time to look for yourself.

Why Use Parables at All?

Beyond the fact that we all understand things differently, we also use the familiar to help us understand new ideas. We often use this device when explaining science. The simple way we draw an atom and speak about the orbits of the electrons uses our familiar planetary solar system to explain something we can't see. We compare them in order to grasp a firm picture in our minds, even if it isn't quite accurate. This type of communication draws from each of our independent experiences. So if you have never seen a model of the solar system, comparing it to an atom may not be helpful.

Sometimes our words carry connotations or meanings that go far beyond the sterile definitions found in dictionaries. These subtle variations in word definitions may vary from person-to-person and even region-to-region. Changes in the meanings derived from words may shift generationally as well, such that the word *bad* may mean *very good* to persons of a certain region and age. These subtle but at times powerful word meanings shift according to our socio-ethnic backgrounds as well.

These obstacles in communication are found within the same language. When you add the complexity of multitudes of languages, the problem of describing a new idea becomes overwhelming. Painting word-pictures are often the only way to introduce new concepts that are completely unfamiliar. We can do this through drawing comparisons, contrasting similarities and differences, and building images inside of our heads to bring the strange into light or understanding. Often, concepts can only be explained using a simile like 'God is the potter and we are the clay', an example found in Isaiah 64, verse 8, or metaphor, such as the "peace like a river" referred to in Isaiah 66, verse 12.

Words receive their meanings from physical objects, our experiences, and the firing of our emotions and senses. We learn our first language by experiencing not by memorizing. We know the word 'chair' as something to sit on from the experience of sitting in the chair or an apple is to eat in the same way. This experience of language can be extended to sense words like cold or hot, red, musty, or even sad. Most of us have experienced these by receiving outside inputs through our sensory receptors and organs. Whether felt through the pressure receptors in our skin, the tiny cilia sitting in the ocean of potassium in our ears, the light absorbing receptors in our retinas, the chemical receptors of our tongues and noses, or the perception of danger in the fear center of our amygdalas, they all cause our neurons to fire messages to our brains for response and filing for future references. This is how our first understanding of language is built through personal experiences. It is really surprising that we can communicate at all with such subjective tools that differ so significantly from person to person. How do we know that the tones of songs or colors are the same for everyone? We know that they vary radically for the tone deaf and the color blind but what about the other senses? Stories share much more than words alone can convey. They build a commonality of emotions that words alone cannot.

Sometimes, the word paintings drawn by comparing and contrasting need to be supplemented with a deeper meaning or lesson. The tool used throughout the Bible to introduce deeper messages is the parable. From references such as not putting new wine into old skins to the story of the woman with the issue of blood touching the hem, we find literary tools to help explain the truths of new ideas and enable shifts in paradigms. The lessons are larger than just a description of the new thing, but they encompass a shift in belief system or assumptions. New ideas introduce emotional concepts that we can only relate to if we can tap into a time that we have somehow felt the same. Imagining a kitten hanging by her claws for dear life is more effective than just saying, "hang in there, baby".

Even with the word-pictures drawn by simile, metaphor and parables, we still can't be sure that we feel the same emotions. Each of us perceives colors, tastes, and smells differently. Word-pictures give us a chance to draw similar conclusions when learning new concepts. Luckily, most humans can relate to another human by way of our special cells called mirror neurons, thus enabling us to share in the emotions of others even as a bystander. This is why we can get so excited by a football game or cry at a sad scene in a movie. Short of being shown, stories that hold universal experiences are the next best thing.

In the Bible, we find that King David, King Solomon, the prophets, Jesus, Paul and others, used these tools. In Matthew 13, verse 3, we are told that Jesus taught many things in story form and in fact, Mark 4 verse 34 told us "He did not say anything to them without using a parable. But when he was alone with his own disciples, he explained everything". We are told in John 10 verse 6, that Jesus used this figure of speech, but they did not understand what he was telling them. Jesus only explained the word-pictures to his closest companions but we are told that even then the apostles didn't understand the ideas he was sharing. Short of performing miracles on everyone, Jesus needed to speak in parables to the crowds. While sharing new principles and ideas, he painted portraits of the familiar in which to compare and contrast the new.

The question now becomes, what new concepts was he teaching? New ideas and hypotheses in physics allow us to take a second look at what he was sharing. Putting aside what we learned in Sunday school and looking with a fresh pair of glasses (to use a metaphor), without assumptions or preconceived ideas, may allow us to uncover a new understanding of his lessons. It may allow us to see the literal concepts inside the word-pictures. These tools may lead us to a deeper understanding about the concepts being shared by these stories. This is not to say that we should disregard the prior interpretations of great minds that have come before, but only that we have the opportunity to look at the Bible in the light of all our newly gained knowledge of the workings of our universe and our bodies.

When we speak of things such as multiple dimensions other than space (length, depth, and width) and time, or introducing new ideas in quantum physics, we need metaphors to aid us in the understanding of the principle. Even though the metaphor may not be exact, it helps to paint a picture of what is going on in the mathematics behind the physics. Why is this important? Imagine explaining what something feels, tastes, smells, or looks like to someone that has never used that sense without simile or metaphor. It would be impossible.

Try to describe how a pear tastes and feels when you eat it. In the movie, City of Angels, Meg Ryan's character described a pear as "sugary sand that melts in your mouth". Pretty nice picture unless you have ever had sand in your mouth, but somehow if the sand melts, the description works. Now try to describe something without using similar things to compare it to. Descriptions of our sensory input are only possible through comparing it to something we have experienced universally.

When we describe things that our senses can't receive, we must use comparison and imagery. Jesus tried to share his understanding of Divine energy and information to us at a time when none had ever heard of sound waves, microwaves, x-rays, radio waves, television, light waves or light particles. Today, waves are taken for granted. We watch our shows, get updates, and conduct business on our cell phones using WiFi at our local coffee house. Can you imagine trying to explain all this to a person that has never used a radio, TV or microwave? We would need to paint a word picture with a story to share how these things work. It is no wonder that stories are used to illustrate a deeper meaning than words can express using their mere definitions. The Bible explained to us how the universal laws worked by telling stories or parables using comparisons and imagery. Matthew told us in chapter 13, verse 34 that Jesus always used stories and illustrations like these when speaking to the crowds. In fact, he never spoke to them without using such parables. He described things that the crowds had never experienced.

We use metaphors and storytelling to explain what our language or understanding hasn't caught up with yet. For an example, how does a scientist explain that a particle of light can be both a wave and a particle at the same time to school age children or most adults for that matter? The scientist uses comparatives that are familiar to the group. We have all seen water curve around rocks and we know that water comes in molecules and droplets. Much like water, when a particle of light hits a small slit or object, it spreads out and bends around the corners at different rates creating a rainbow effect. We can see this spreading out with electrons and protons too. Does this mean that any particle of matter is made of both waves and particles? In the field of quantum physics, when we break down matter to its smallest component, vibrating waves of light are found. Of course, these are not complete pictures. But, these word-pictures, using water and light, are the simplest ways of explaining how something can be both a particle and a wave considering that most of us don't understand even simple calculus.

God, the Universe, and a Time for Plain Talk

In John 16, verse 25, Jesus confided to us "Though I have been speaking figuratively, a time is coming when I will no longer use this kind of language but will tell you plainly about my Father". We are living in the time when we can understand the ideas and truths in literal connotations! It is time for the plain talk that Jesus spoke about and time to revisit the stories many of us learned as children for a clearer understanding of God, the universe, and ourselves.

The first story accounted in the Bible is the creation story. In Genesis, God said, "Let there be light". There are two important parts to this statement regarding the creation of the universe. The first is that God spoke. The second is the beginning of light. Both are important.

The word *spoke* in our translations of the Bible is from the Greek word, *logos*. Logos doesn't only mean *spoke*, it is also the root of the word logic so it can mean a sound, a word or the principle that gives order and rationality to the universe. The Bible tells us that God spoke. He sent out a sound wave, the first sound wave! In actuality, these waves are fluctuations in pressure. This wave describes the force that began our universe in a way that we can understand. The energy of that first wave then began light. Our universe is filled with energy waves. Could it be that the meaning of logos could be a metaphor for the energy waves that make up matter? Microwaves, radio waves, and even electricity are relatively new discoveries. Even now, how does one explain electricity or even a radio to someone that has never heard of them? We can explain them using comparisons of common things we know, such as sound, light or water waves.

It is easy to understand why sound waves were used to explain the invisible energy around us. One of the simplest energy waves to understand is a sound wave. We know that the compression waves of sound push air molecules into each other creating movement of energy while leaving the individual molecules behind. We see this transmission of force when we hit a cue ball or one billiard ball into another, forcing the second ball into action and leaving the first ball stopped. Compression waves are also found in the movement of earthquakes and ocean waves. The universe began building stars and planets through a process called accretion, or the crashing together of particles that fused together creating larger and larger parts. Is it possible that 'Logos' was used to explain the energy waves that spread out and formed the universe? The metaphor of sound waves is a great way to explain the energy that formed of the universe.

Logos is used many times in the Bible to describe the beginnings of the universe. In John 1 verse 1, we are told, "In the beginning was the Word (logos), and the Word was with God, and the Word was God". This literally means that sound, a metaphor for energy, existed before the beginning of the universe, existed with God, and was itself God. The energy that created a word, a sound wave, existed before the beginning of our universe, was with God, and was God. This verse told us that this Divine energy permeates everything that exists.

The second part of Genesis 1, verse 3 is God spoke, "Let there be light". The translation from Greek actually means, "Let light exist". This light or energy wave existed before the stars or our sun were created! Is light being used as a second metaphor for explaining energy? Up until that instance, only God existed and he started an energy wave that propagated more forces, much the same way that light moves through space propagating electric and magnetic fields.

According to Einstein, light doesn't need a matrix to move through. Of course, there is a matrix of energy and empty space is anything but empty. Einstein believed that light moved in a type of wavy dance through space. He explained that this vibration of an electromagnetic charge creates the electric field. This electric field creates a perpendicular magnetic field, which creates another electric field that creates another magnetic field, and so on, vibrating along, field creating field spreading out across space. Light waves dance through space, spiraling and vibrating between their electric and magnetic components until they are absorbed or reflected by other particles or interfered with by other waves. On the tiniest of quantum levels, everything is made up of vibrations of light popping in and out of existence. We know this by watching the paths of colliding particles going in and out of existence within a particle accelerator such as the one found at the CERN (Council on European Nuclear Research), on the Franco-Swiss border in Geneva. CERN is also the birthplace of the Worldwide Web.

Light is energy and light creates energy. We know that God is not simply visible light. Conversely, it doesn't mean that darkness is the absence of God. Visible light is just a small part of the spectrum of electromagnetic energy. We can't see ultra-violet or infrared waves, which are very close to the spectrum we can see. Outside of the visible wavelengths lay X-rays, microwaves, radio waves and all of the familiar waves of electromagnetic fields. According to quantum physics, everything is formed with waves and particles, and the interactions or forces between these waves and particles. When Jesus said, "I am the light of the world" in John 8 verse 12, could he have been speaking both figuratively and literally? Figuratively, light is a metaphor for understanding and a guide, but the literal sensibility is that Jesus is made up of particles, waves, and forces that powerfully interact to create matter.

Divine Energy is All Powerful, All Knowing, and Always Present

Now that we understand the necessity of using stories, descriptions and other such word-pictures, we can begin to decipher the mental images found in parables, in hopes of finding the literal meanings that science gives us the opportunity to understand.

Is God Infinite Energy?

The prophet Isaiah, in chapter 40, verse 28 told us "His power" or energy "is absolute or unending". Where can we find this kind of unending force? In 1913, Albert Einstein and Otto Stern suggested the existence of an enduring energy in empty space called zero-point energy. In 1948, a Dutch physicist named Hendrik B. G. Casimir predicted the existence of a powerful energy or force in the vacuum of empty space or the figurative heavens. This prediction waited until 1996 to be proven. Steve Lamoreaux at Los Alamos National Laboratory in New Mexico proved that infinite energy exists in what we think of as empty space. Subsequent experiments have proven that empty space between very near objects, spaces as tiny as only 100 atoms, produce a force that is equivalent to 1 atmosphere of pressure or pressure we feel at sea level. That is a huge amount of force in a very small, and alleged empty, space! And, this energy is present everywhere, even in the emptiness of space.

Since this is such a tiny amount of space, scientists had to sum up this energy for the whole universe. They added it up for all the different parts the universe and their harmonic responses. A harmonic response is much like the movement of a tuning fork or string causing other tuning forks or strings to vibrate.

The vibrations of the zero-point force cause other vibrations, which cause more vibrations and so on. Scientists were trying to add up the total amount of energy in the universe. Scientific America reported in the June 22, 1998 edition, "that when this force is added up, the measured energy is infinite". The energy in empty space or the figurative heavens is infinite, like God!

What is even more interesting is that scientists are trying to harness this energy for our use. It is called zero-point energy. NASA published a chapter reviewing the evidence and plausibility of using the energy of empty space in NASA: Advanced Energetics for Aeronautical Application Volume II in 2005. Scientists hope to power our lights, transportation and everything on the harmonic energy found in empty space. In both the sixth chapter of Isaiah and the twenty-first chapter of Revelations, we are told that we will no longer need the sun, the moon, or lamps because the Divine will give us light. Figuratively, light can mean *understanding* but when we harness zero-point energy, we will be able to interpret these verses literally and run our cities on the free energy of the Divine Universe. Scientists are now testing crystal harmonic resonance to harness the energy of empty space to utilize it as renewable energy.

Believe it or not, we already make use of crystals to generate electricity. Lighters use piezoelectric crystals to light fires. When struck, the crystal deforms and moves electrons generating electricity. Guitars and Basses can use tiny piezoelectric crystals called piezo-pickups under their strings to send electricity to the amplifier and speakers. We are very close to utilizing the Divine Energy of the universe to power our cities. There is more power in zero-point energy than we will ever be able to use. No more running out of nonrenewable resources or not being able to afford to heat our homes. The Divine Energy of the universe will never run out.

If space contains so much, why can't we see it? How is it possible that empty space contains an infinite amount of energy while solid matter contains less energy? The image that I like to use is that of water. When water is liquid, it is denser than when it is solid. Proof of this is the fact that ice floats on the top of water allowing fish and other water creatures to remain in the water under the ice. Brilliant really. When water begins to freeze, its molecules line up so that hydrogen bonds are formed in ranks like small soldiers spacing themselves out arm-to-arm and no closer. These bonds hold the molecules apart with their force. Like the negative ends of little magnets, the forces repel the molecules of solid ice further apart than the molecules in liquid water, which are free to move around. When we see ice, we see solid matter, but liquid water is in reality denser. Of course, we are only using a metaphor to explain how it could happen since matter is in actual fact 99.9999999999999 percent empty space. So really, everything contains a lot of space, including ourselves, and we don't perceive empty space in our bodies either. (Does this mean we could house 99.9999999999999 percent Divine Energy?) Of course, we can't see most energy because most energy is not within the visible spectrum of light and that is why we don't see the radio waves, microwaves or x-rays either. Just like fish in water, we are swimming in an ocean of energy. Is this why we don't see God?

Another thought on why the energy of the universe goes mostly undetected is explained by the Heisenberg's Uncertainty Principle. This principle states that just watching something will change it or interfere with it. This principle also states that when trying to measure something infinitesimal like a photon or electron, the smaller or tighter the measurement, the less precise the results, because the measurement will change it. Try throwing a marble through a hole. The smaller or tighter the hole is, the greater the alteration in the path of the marble when it comes out the other side. This happens because the marble bounces off the sides of the hole. But, if we want to know the exact size of the marble, we must use smaller and smaller holes. So the principle says: the more precise the measurement, the tighter we must clamp down, and the more we change the thing we are measuring. When something is very small and very fast, we must measure it very quickly. Just like when cars collide, more speed equals more force and more damage to the cars, or the marbles. When we try to measure the energy of the heavens, the energy fluctuations of the universe pop in and out of existence almost instantaneously, so we have very little time to measure the energy. These fleeting waves in the universal ocean are called virtual photons. These virtual photons are the building blocks of everything! It was almost impossible to measure the magnitudes of these incredibly short-lived vibrations of energy so it seems like there was no energy in empty space. This is why scientists couldn't measure it until now.

According to Physicist Stephen Hawking, today's scientists believe that the universe began with a single point in time and space: a singularity, a point containing infinite energy. Genesis tells us, "In the beginning, God created the heavens and the earth." The universe was created out of the only thing that there was or will ever be, infinite energy. Steven Hawking tells us that the universe has not existed forever and that its beginning can be traced back to one point. Scientists trace this by looking through very powerful telescopes like the Hubble Space Telescope. Cosmologists at places like the Arecibo Observatory can measure the speed, direction and distance that the different stars are traveling. They can extrapolate back to the point and time that the stars all exploded from. At the time of the singularity, all energy and matter would have been united. The density of energy at this point would be infinite. This point is called a singularity and the entire universe came from it. A singularity is created when the quantity of one thing gets bigger and bigger heading towards infinity while something related decreases towards zero. An example of this would be, as mass goes to zero, energy gets infinitely larger. The singularity at the beginning of the universe started at the place where mass was zero and energy was infinite. Before the beginning, all that existed was infinite energy.

God, who already existed as infinity, just like the singularity before the Big Boom, created the heavens and the earth. In Romans 11, verse 36 we are told, "For from him and through him and to him are all things." The singularity that Dr. Hawking speaks of is the infinite energy through which all things began. The universe was made from pure energy and the first law of thermodynamics tells us that "energy can neither be created nor destroyed", only converted. The energy that created the universe is eternal.

Hawking tells us that the point of energy that created the universe was infinitely dense. He also believes that due to the curved nature of the universe it continues forever. The gravitational force of something infinitely dense curves space, much like placing a heavy bowling ball in the middle of a waterbed or a heavy person on a trampoline. They curve the surfaces. The heavier the object, the more the surface curves. The universe has no end. Its like traveling on the inside of a sphere or on a mobius strip, it doesn't end. For those that aren't familiar with a mobius strip, just take a piece of flat ribbon, twist it once in the middle and tape the ends together. Now you can move along both sides of the ribbon without end. So, the universe is infinite and unending.

This sounds like the description of the eternal God. Let's see, science tells us the universal energy began everything, is everything, and is never ending. Hmm? Isaiah 40, verse 28 said, "the everlasting God created earth" and John 1, verse 3, told us that "through him all things were made; without him nothing was made that has been made." Clearly, this is not to say that God is the universe but only that the universe is part of God, much like a piece of cake is part of the whole but not the whole cake. Those cake pieces can be cut in all kinds of shapes but they are still made of cake. Scientists agree that the singularity existed before the universe began. Divine Energy created the universe but is not merely the universe.

Does God Know Everything?

Another important thing to understand about the energy that exists in space is that it contains infinite amounts of information. The energy waves that we use but don't see include radio waves, microwaves, television waves, x-rays, sound, some light, etc. These waves all carry information. We transmit data in the form of bits, music, pictures, and voices, just to name a few uses. Whether in discrete digital packets or in analog waves, the information is carried by electromagnetic energy. Infinite energy carries all of this information. Isaiah tells us that we can't even fathom the information or understanding God contains.

Because infinite energy exists, there are infinite sizes of wavelengths. We still haven't discovered all of the forms of energy and information, or how to use them. In Psalms 139, David describes God's thoughts or understanding as being as infinite as the grains of sand. He explains God as containing all information and as being present everywhere, all of the time. This sounds like the universal field as described by quantum physics.

Virtual particles come in and out of existence and communicate with their entangled partners across space without regard for space and time. Even electrons have an apparent ability to know their partner's condition instantaneously even over vast spaces. This ability is known as nonlocality and was first written about by Einstein, Boris

Podolsky and Nathan Rosen. Einstein called this 'spooky action at a distance' and today we are just beginning to use the capabilities of quantum entanglement to send messages and particles across distances with immediate responses on the other end. Nonlocality shows us that what we believe to be separate in the material universe just isn't separate. Our universe is intimately and instantaneously connected. The quantum universe openly demonstrates that one unified energy source is "in everything, through everything, and holds everything together" just like the Bible told us in Colossians 1, verses 16 and 17.

Everything, including ourselves, is mostly empty space where virtual particles are constantly appearing and disappearing, coming in and out of existence. We are filled with Divine Energy. II Corinthians 4, verse 18 instructed us to look on things that are unseen because the things we can see are temporary and the unseen is eternal. We share infinite, eternal, unseen energy with all things. Only temporary matter can be seen.

The Body Temple

Paul told us in I Corinthians chapter 6, verses 19 and 20, "Your body is a temple of the Holy Spirit within you, whom you have from God". So why is it important to know that your body is a temple of the Holy Spirit? It is a word-picture that tells you who you are. It tells you how to see yourself and gives you an identity, a fundamental belief about yourself. Your body is a temple of the Holy Spirit! Not just any old house but a cathedral of the Divine. Do you really believe that? Can you really get your head and heart around what this means? Imagine how you would treat your body if you truly believed that it was a temple of the Holy Spirit, a sacred place for God.

We have already seen that Divine Energy permeates everything and unites everything. Making this fact personal really changes everything. What would you do differently if you truly believed that your body was the place that the Holy Spirit came to live or exist in? Would you have more respect for the body that God gave you to take care of? The Holy Spirit is the part of God that is used to communicate and visit with each of us. Do you welcome him into his home in your physical being? Just visualize what your house looks like now and how it would look if you knew for certain that God was coming to visit. Would you swing open the doors wide with a smile and wave God in? I don't know about your house but mine would need a complete overhaul! Maybe I would give it a new coat of paint and fresh flowers. I would get new plumbing fixtures and fix the wiring in that lamp that flickers and screw in a new energy efficient bulb. At the very least, I would make sure it was as clean as I could get it and in good repair.

How about your body, the physical vessel that God gave you to live in and to commune with him in; how have you taken care of it? Does it need an overhaul too? What kind of changes do you need to make? Would you clean up and make some repairs? Try to imagine what your body would be like if you truly believed that it was a place that God came to live with you. Picture it in your mind. What would it look like? Would you be healthier? Would you be in better shape? Would you be more joyful and calm? Would you still be taking all of the medications that you are on or eating all of that fast food? Does your body feel and look differently in your mind's eye? Now picture the Holy Spirit inside of the body that you just imagined. How beautiful and full of light your body would be. Can you visualize that body? Now step inside it. It is you! That is your identity. That beautiful, enlightened entity is you.

John told us in chapter 6 verse 63, that Jesus said, "The Spirit gives life; the flesh counts for nothing". If the flesh counts for nothing why is it important to maintain it? We are made in his image, to house him, and for his pleasure. Giving our bodies and our lives the respect they deserve is essential to maintaining our health. What we believe about ourselves is extraordinarily vital to our mental and physical health! We are told in Genesis 6, verse 3, "My Spirit will not strive with man forever, because he also is flesh, yet his days be one hundred twenty years." We are given 120 years of life. The old joke "if I had known that I would live this long, I would have taken better care of myself" becomes a truth. No one wants to live a sick and unhappy existence. The gift of material life is 120 years long. How to live them and fulfill the purpose of being God's pleasure is written for us all to follow.

The Scriptures tell us we are made in his image. This means we are made from the only thing that exists, pure energy; the same infinitely dense energy that existed before the creation of the universe. Quantum physics illuminates the same truth. We are made from particles springing from the infinite energy field that exists everywhere in the universe. We are made of God energy. Much the same way as when you cut and take a piece from an apple, you know that the piece is going to be an apple because that is what it came from. The same energy that brought this universe into existence is the energy that makes you. Its interactions hold you together, and run through you making your heart beat and your cells communicate. No matter what shape you cut the piece of apple into, the content is always what you started with. You are a piece of Universal Energy! It is time we start treating our bodies as the holy temples they are.

Colossians 1, verse 17 told us, "God existed before all things and in him all things hold together". The universal energy field creates waves and particles, which attract and repel each other. The Divine Force of the universe holds us together with interactions so intimate that we don't even take notice of it. Just grab a car radio antenna or an old-fashioned television antenna and note how much better the clarity of the music or the picture is when your hand is on it. The static electricity in the air interacts with us. While bringing some laundry in, I noticed the static electricity caused the fringe of a towel to stand straight up. Waving my hand just above it, I watched the fringe follow my hand back and forth. My little cha-weenie dog, Neo became curious and stuck his nose into the area near my hand and all of the fringe came to a point and touched his nose. The energy seemed to look at him as he looked at it. The field interacts with everything all the time. Sometimes a painful shock of static electricity reminds us to pay attention.

Am I saying that we are God? No! Emphatically no! Is the apple seed the apple? No, but it is given creative power. The Bible tells us in Matthew chapters 8 and 17, that we are given the power to do anything including moving mountains, and stopping the wind and the waves. We are the apple seed but not the whole essence of the apple. This is why it is so important to realize what we are. It is like the pauper that doesn't know he's a prince. He begs. It is only with the knowledge of his royal birthright that he begins to act in respect and dignity. David, in Psalm 139, gave thanks to God for making us "fearfully and wonderfully". Luke 11, verse 36 quoted Jesus as saying our bodies are full of light, a simple metaphor to explain that we are vibrating energy. Light is a dance or oscillation in the electromagnetic field. We are the dance of life in an invisible ocean of energy. We should live knowing that we share this energy with God and each other. This fact is enough to revolutionize how we treat others and ourselves.

According to Quantum physics, at our smallest level, we are all made of the interactions between light vibrations. In Matthew five, verse 14, Jesus said, "You are the light of the world." Why would you want to hide your brilliant energy? Let the Divine energy shine through you to light up every room you walk in. The Bible gives us instructions on how to shine bright with joy, health and vitality.

Faith and the Photon

As temples of the Holy Spirit, we have been powerfully made in the image of God. We can fashion the world around us. We are told that all we need is the faith of a mustard seed and a mountain will get up and move. Science concurs with this belief but to understand how, we need to know a little about light. Light has properties of both waves and particles. We know this because of a famous double slit experiment by the French physicist, Louis de Brolie. He sent speeding photons or light particles through two small slits or openings to a sheet of receiving media such as film in back of the slits. If photons acted like particles they would hit the media directly behind the slits like balls thrown through two holes at a wall. They would hit the same spots over and over. This did not happen! The speeding photons spread out to form a pattern of vertical lines across the receiving media instead of just hitting directly behind the opening. This pattern proves that photons act like waves. We all have seen a wave of water go around a rock or pier and we expect to hear the sound of each other's voices from around a corner. Waves go around corners. Sometimes when light hits an object it makes rainbow colored lines on a wall. This happens because particles of light also form waves of light. The different light waves spread out, either adding together to increase intensity or brightness much like many streams add up to make a mighty river, or they collide with each other, canceling each other out and causing darkness. This is why the light on the wall forms lines of color alternating with lines of darkness. It doesn't form a solid beam of light when going through slits or around objects. Louis de Brolie showed that both electrons and protons responded in the same fashion. And, that all particles have a wavelength and a frequency including our bodies.

The amazing thing about this experiment is this; if photons are observed while speeding towards the slits, they act like particles and do hit the media directly behind the slits. This happens anytime we watch or try to detect the position or mass of things because we add interference to the system. We can change things just by observing them. Niels Bohr, a Swedish Nobel prizewinner for his work on atomic structure, hypothesized that the properties of waves and particles are not intrinsic to the light itself but are dependent on human observation or interaction, and depend on what the observer wants to see. Photons choose to be particles or waves depending on whether human participation is involved. Many other scientists concur.

Dr. John Wheeler, an American physicist that worked with Niels Bohr and collaborated with Einstein (though he and

Einstein didn't always agree), wrote that we don't just observe the universe but actually participate in it. Just by the act of observing the universe, we change it, at least from the point of our perspective. Genesis 1, verse 27 announced that, we are made in God's image. In Matthew 21, verse 21, we are told that mountains will fall into the sea if we tell them to move. Science may be telling us the same thing. We participate in changing our world merely by observing it. This concept is called the Heisenberg's Uncertainty Principle. The German physicist, Werner Heisenberg concluded that when we observe small particles of matter, we affect their behavior. This happens regardless of how hard we try not to disrupt objects in experiments. We are like a kid standing in the dark at the edge of a cliff. If we throw a stone down it to see how long it takes to hit the bottom, we may be able to tell its depth by the amount of time it takes. Unfortunately, the stone needs to be large enough to resonate a noise loud enough to be heard at the top and it may crush the person at the bottom looking up. So we know something about the depth but have changed the thing we are observing by crushing the person at the bottom. This always happens. We are interacting with and not just watching the universe all of the time. The faith to move mountains becomes easy when we believe what science and the Bible tell us about ourselves; we can change our world!

One Infinite Energy Field, One Divine Spirit

Today, we know that we share our most fundamental parts with everything else in the universe. Our electrons and other, even smaller particles, are exchanging at a tremendous rate. Our bodies are renewing on a quantum level, atomic level, and cellular level all of the time. Some of our electrons are trading places with everything around us at a very rapid pace. The protons and neutrons in the nucleus of our atoms are made up of smaller particles named quarks. Quarks are pulled together by power particles called gluons that are constantly popping in and out of existence from the infinite field. When we think of powers that hold everything together, we think of forces like gravity or quantum level forces, not power particles like gluons that appear and disappear faster than we can blink. The infinite field produces particles including power particles like gluons and photons constantly. These particles are excitements in the field that interact causing ripples of varying frequencies and wavelengths. Imagine a very small, very violent mosh (slam-dancing) pit where the collisions cause the dancers to disappear and reappear doing a different dance. We can't see this virtual dance but Nobel prizewinner Dr. Richard Feynman gave us a way to visualize the pathways of subatomic particles. Sometimes they are even going backwards in time.

Steven Hawking has worked out the calculations that allow a virtual particle from the energy field of empty space to become real. Virtual particles twinkle in and out of existence almost instantaneously and almost always appear as a pair. The pair, one particle and its antiparticle, immediately collide and annihilate each other, but if a pair of virtual particles appears in the vicinity of a black hole and one of the pair is pulled into the black hole, the other is no longer in danger of annihilation and may stabilize as a real particle. Real and virtual particles come from the so-called empty vacuum of space and return to it, appearing and disappearing, sharing and interacting. With this much coming, going and exchanging from the Divine Energy field, it is surprising that we have as much illness as we do.

All matter is merely a very dense traffic jam of the interactions between quantum particles, held together by energy or the quantum field. You share what you are with the whole universe. The universal energy field creates and recreates everything from the same stuff. No matter where we find a proton, electron or photon, each one is always exactly the same! We are the one Spirit and one body written about in

Ephesians 4. In Ecclesiastes 3 verse 19, Solomon declared that it is vanity to think that we are superior to animals because we share one breath. We are all made up of infinite energy and share it with everyone and everything, whether we think of it as being alive or not. Living sponges are primarily silicon-based and so are the rocks of the earth. Is it so far-fetched to imagine that consciousness is shared with all things whether carbon-based or silicon-based? Maybe the rocks really do cry out and praise God as spoke of in Luke 19 verse 40. If we are nothing but patterns of interactions between quantum particles and we are conscious of ourselves, why is it hard to believe that the infinite energy and singularity that produced the entire universe might be the conscious Holy Spirit as well? Maybe what Carl Jung called the 'collective unconscious' is simply God.

We are eternal spirit in a temple or material body. In Revelations 3, verse 16, Jesus warned us to be hot or cold, not lukewarm. We are to live passionately! Why are we here? John answered that question in Revelations 4, verse eleven, "God created all things and for God's pleasure all things are here". We are here for God's pleasure. We are the vessels through which the Divine Energy experiences life, all the good and bad, hot and cold, pain and pleasure. As vessels of the Holy Spirit, we have a responsibility to maintain our vessels for God's pleasure.

Caring for God's Temple

The Bible has directions for taking care of our bodies with food, herbs, recreation, prayer and meditation. We read these instructions but don't really take them seriously. In 1 Corinthians 3:16-17 we are warned, "Don't you know that you yourselves are God's temple and that God's Spirit lives in you? If anyone destroys God's temple, God will destroy him; for God's temple is sacred, and you are that temple". We see destruction in the form of cancers, heart disease, diabetes, obesity and other avoidable diseases. It is time to care for our bodies as if they are sacred. We are also told that our bodies are not our own. In 1 Corinthians 6:19, "Do you not know that your body is a temple of the Holy Spirit, who is in you, whom you have received from God? You are not your own". We have received our bodies from God but how do we properly care for these magnificent temples?

In the past, scientists observed improvements in health caused by certain herbs or foods, but couldn't find a reason for them. The positive results were chalked up to a placebo effect. But, what causes the placebo effect? The choices we make, the environment we live in, the beliefs and attitudes we hold, the relationships and recreation we participate in, each control how our gene code is copied into proteins, enzymes and other factors. These proteins manage all of our bodily functions whether growth, maintenance or decline. The study of the mechanisms that can alter the way our genetic code is used without changing our underlying DNA is called epigenetics. The epi prefix is defined as *above* and of course, genetics means the study of our genes, so epigenetics is the study of how a new layer of control, above the DNA manages our genetic code. Actually, the study of epigenetics has been around for over twenty years so it's not really new.

By hanging different molecular groups on and around the parts that make up our chromosomes, epigenetic mechanisms can vary the ways we copy DNA to assemble amino acids. Amino acids are used to construct the building blocks that construct and maintain our bodies. Epigenetic mechanisms influence which proteins are made, their amounts and even the shapes they are folded into. These molecular groups act like little magnets, attracting and repelling electrons in order to adjust how our genes are utilized. They are the source of the transformations that cause each of our stem cells to differentiate into the different types of cells that make up all of our bodies' systems.

Epigenetic mechanisms are the reasons why identical twins' health can vary even from the first hours after birth. It explains why one twin can become diabetic or develop cancer while the other remains healthy. Merely altering the blood supply of identical twins sharing the same cord and placenta can result in one twin developing metabolic diseases later in life and not the other. Dr. Randy Jirtle and his colleagues found that improving the nutrition of rat pups before or directly after birth can alleviate negative traits from developing. Nutrients aren't the only things that affect epigenetic mechanisms. Dr. Jirtle found that giving the pups nutrients could also alleviate certain negative traits caused by environmental toxins. Human trials have shown similar results.

In 1944, an isolated community in Western Holland suffered from starvation. Historical records of the starvation enabled scientists to follow the consequences of being pregnant and malnourished during different phases of gestation and how this affected their offspring. After following several generations, results show that not only the mother but also the father and the grandparents can cause inheritable alterations in the health of our offspring. What we do today not only causes changes in the way our bodies use their genetic codes but also affects our children's and grandchildren's epigenetic mechanisms. Epigenetic mechanisms control whether we suffer from cancer, rheumatism and many other age related diseases. We were given power over our genetic codes from the beginning. Now we can follow the directions contained in the Scriptures knowing they have lasting consequences affecting our mental, emotional and physical health. In most cases, the environment commands how our genes are used over 70% of the time. It seems that in the battle between nature and nurture, nurture wins out almost three to one. The Bible instructs us how to nurture ourselves in order to enhance our epigenetic health using belief or faith, vegetation, fasting, philanthropy, recreation, praise, prayer and meditation. For instance, in Revelation 22, verse 2 and Ezekiel 47, verse 12, we are told that the fruits of the trees will be food and the leaves of the trees will be for medicine.

Today scans of the brain and body, combined with measurements such as monitoring the heart, body temperature, respiratory and pulse rates, offer insights into how our brains can control and engage our bodies. New tests measure changes in the amounts of methyl, acetyl and other groups attached to our DNA. Knowing the quantity of methyl groups and other groups attached to our genomic machinery helps scientists observe how epigenetics can control alterations in our health and happiness. Experimentation on yeasts, insects, animals and humans has increased understanding of how our environment affects the use of DNA and how enriched environments can be utilized to enhance health. The bottom line is this: what we believe, and how we act and react affect the copying of our genetic code. The benefits and consequences of following or not following Biblical advice can be observed in the state of our health and well-being.

Imaging such as magnetic resonance imaging (MRI) and positron emission tomography (PET) allow us to see inside a person's brain, while they are alive and functioning, to track their growth, damage and repair. Deep prayer and meditation can cause new neural growth in the brain. Singing praises and doing good deeds increase the amounts of neurotransmitters and endorphins in our brains, enhancing our happiness and diminishing our stress, anxiety and pain.

The most critical ingredients to good health are our beliefs and perceptions about the world around us. Stress is one of the main causes of the wearing down of our bodies. Whether the stress is emotional or physical, the body reacts as if it needs to physically protect us. Stress is fine when we live in danger of being eaten by wild animals, but today most stresses are mental. The hormones that are released, due to today's mental stresses aren't usually dissipated by running from or fighting the danger, so the stressful state lingers. We can't simply run away from our thoughts and reactions. This state of hyper-alertness drains our reserves and makes us more vulnerable to illness and genetic errors. Modern stress is perceived stress. Unlike the wild lion at the door, the proverbial lion is one constructed of ideas, beliefs and assumptions. Pressures built with erroneous attitudes are killing us.

Chronic stress leads to anxiety and depression. King Solomon knew that "A cheerful heart is good medicine but a broken spirit dries up the bones". Stress saps our strength. When we are told to praise in song and serve others, we are shown ways to strengthen our bodies by increasing the chemicals that ensure a sense of well-being. How we perceive the things that are happening around us, in other words, how we believe, think and emotionally respond to what is occurring, dictates what chemicals are created in our bodies and how they perform.

If we look around, we can see how the sins of the fathers and mothers affect the children with their unhealthy eating habits, anxious attitudes, and couch potato habits. Today's children are heavier and sicker than ever before. The Center for Disease Control and Prevention reported that childhood obesity has more than tripled in the past 30 years. Over one third of children and adolescents between the ages of 5 to 17-years-old are overweight or obese. Up to 70 percent of obese children show risk factors for cardiovascular diseases like high blood pressure or high cholesterol. Our children deserve better.

We are not stuck with the diseases and chronic problems that are caused by these habits and attitudes. The body and brain can repair themselves. It takes 6 to 12 months to repair the receptors and neurotransmitters that cause cravings, but only if we follow the instructions. Less than 30 percent of people diagnosed with diabetes, asthma, elevated blood pressure, heart disease or obesity follow the suggestions their doctors give them and make the changes needed to heal and recover. When we follow the Biblical command to fast, it resets of the amounts of neurotransmitters needed to energize receptors. This rebooting of our brains and bodies can help free us from cravings and other addictions. Galatians 5, verse 1 said, "It is for freedom that Christ has set us free. Stand firm, then, and do not let yourselves be burdened again by a yoke of slavery." We can become free from the addictions of food and drink, and free from depression and anxiety. In Mark 9, verses 28 and 29, the disciples asked Jesus why only he could heal the mentally ill man. Jesus answered that "only by fasting and prayer" does mental illness leave. Fasting and meditation helps change our brains and its chemistry.

Why is the success rate so low? When one stops a behavior, food or drug, it leaves a gaping empty space. If you don't fill that hole with something nurturing or healthy, the addictive substance or something equally harmful will fill it. Divine instructions tell us how to fill it and what to fill it with. Studies have shown us how faith, good deeds, singing and dancing, prayer and meditation, and especially fasting can help us to positively and permanently change behaviors and addictions. Healing and recovery is as easy as following the simple, straightforward instructions found in the Scriptures.

These instructions and more are found in the verses that we studied and memorized as children. Ephesians 4, verse 24, told us, "and to put on the new self, created to be like God in true righteousness and holiness." You are a temple of the Spirit of the Divine. You can create a new temple, healthy and ready to welcome the Holy Spirit. Paul said in Ephesians chapter 6, verse 10, "Finally, be strong in the Lord and in his mighty power". All the power you need to purify your temple is already in you and ready to be accessed by you. The Bible and epigenetics agree. All you need to do is follow the directions that are found in the Scriptures.

Sciences, including medicine, genetics, cellular biology, and physics have combined to contribute to a new understanding of how following simple biblical principles can aid in our health and happiness. Much more than we ever imagined, we have the knowledge to change how we feel both physically and emotionally, even if we believe right now that we can never change. Having faith as small as a mustard seed and choosing to follow the instructions are all that is necessary.

We Are Temples of Light

Physicists tell us a point of infinitely dense energy called a singularity created the universe, but how does that energy create our bodies, our world and the multitudes of universes? Scientists still don't completely understand what makes up the forces that hold our universe together. They have names for the force that holds the nucleus of atoms together and names for the force that makes radioactive materials fall apart, but they don't have proof of how or why these forces work. We are told in Colossians 1, verse 17, "He existed before everything and that in him all things are held together". The singularity existed before the universe, still exists and the entire universe is constructed "in" its energy fields. This infinite power created the universe and everything in it. What do you believe? Is the infinite singularity that created everything what we call God?

How is it that we are nothing but energy? Though we perceive a world of solids, liquids and occasionally gases, physicists, and even Einstein realize that all states of matter are traffic jams of energy. Because we experience these states differently with our senses, we identify them as something other than energy. One of the reasons for this is the sensation of heaviness. Our physical world has mass. When mass interacts with gravity gives us the measurement of weight but what is mass? Over a hundred years ago in 1905, Einstein identified a new energy. This was the energy of mass itself. He said that mass acts like a super concentrated cluster of energy, or rather bunches of energy act like mass. In other words, mass is energy! A simplified version of Einstein's famous formula is

$E=MC^2$ or energy equals the speed of light multiplied the speed of light, which is then multiplied by the mass.

For over one hundred years, science has known that energy turns into mass and mass can turn into energy. They are exchangeable; just accelerate at twice the speed of light. Implied in this formula is the understanding that as a particle of mass gets going faster and faster, the mass gets larger and the energy it takes to move it becomes infinitely large. Things feel heavier, or more massive, the faster they go. We all experience this phenomenon while riding in a fast car or on a roller coaster. Plastered back against the seat while accelerating quickly, we feel increased heaviness. Acceleration creates the feeling of heaviness or what we call weight. According to Einstein, we must have movement to have mass. Of course, we are in motion on a planet that's in motion, in a solar system that is in motion, etc. If we go smaller we find that our cells, molecules, atoms, electrons, photons, and smaller are constantly in motion too. This motion creates the sensation of weight or mass in our universe of energy.

Proof that mass and energy are interchangeable is demonstrated with the neutron bomb. If particles are accelerating very rapidly, they have a lot of forward moving energy. And, like speeding cars crashing to a halt, it takes a huge amount of energy to stop them. When a sufficient amount of neutrons, inside a radioactive material, starts speeding around and colliding, it creates a huge amount of energy. This energy can generate huge explosions like the bombs dropped in WWII. Sufficient accelerating mass crashing into each other could create enough energy to annihilate our world, and this is just a minuscule amount of the energy available in the infinite energy field!

It is easy to see how mass becomes energy just by watching a fire burning wood to generate the energy of heat, but scientists still don't fully understand exactly how energy becomes mass. Scientists are still searching for how energy acquires mass or weight and how our bodies or any other physical objects formed. Dr. Peter Higgs and 5 other physicists postulated that the Higgs' boson (Yes, that is what they call it. They also call it "the God particle") could be the particle that accumulates mass on other particles. On March 13, 2013, scientists thought they found the boson. A collision of two protons in the Large Hadron Collider at CERN left a signature, or type of trail, that acted the way they think a boson particle should act. The boson may or may not cause other particles to acquire mass. They don't know yet and a lot more research is needed to prove it either way.

Some scientists are looking for different explanations. Einstein is quoted as saying "what we have called matter is energy, whose vibration has been so lowered as to be perceptible to the senses. There is no matter". Other scientists agree. They believe that mass is just a super-concentrated interaction of energy fields in the vacuum of space. Some scientist such as Nassim Haramein, Elizabeth Rauscher and Michael Hyson, even believe that tiny black holes suck energy into one side of the field and push out condensed particles on the other side.

Two scientists, working at California State University at Long Beach, Alfonso Rueda and Bernard Haisch, are looking for the reason particles have mass. Dr. Haisch believes that mass is due to the interactions between the basic building blocks of matter, which are called particles, and the energy of so-called empty space. While trying to harness the energy of empty space to use as free power, scientists have come to believe that mass is only wild interactions acting like the waves in a storm. What we perceive as matter is a traffic jam of energy slowed down enough that we can perceive it. The infinite energy of emptiness or what scientists call zero-point energy creates everything.

Einstein knew that mass and energy were interchangeable. All mass comes into existence and returns to energy, or Spirit, whether it's the mass of an atom or the whole mass of our bodies. Energy forms particles, waves and their interactions, which are the simple building blocks that construct our material world. The parts may be simple but how and why they are put together still boggles us. Colossians 1, verse 16 explained, "all things were created by God, through God and for God". At first this sounds a little redundant but the universe was created 'by' the singularity, 'through' the zero-point energy of the singularity and 'for' the pleasure of a conscious being, the singularity. Webster's defines spirit as: "an animating or vital principle held to give life to physical organisms". Science has defined the essence or Spirit of the universe as an infinite point of energy that existed before the universe and endures in empty space. Is this the Holy Spirit?

Mass is perceived due to interactions in the Heavens. The Heavens or the empty vacuum of space is an invisible, churning sea of vibrating and interacting energy fields. These stormy wave-like fields are called zero-point fluctuations and they create tiny whirlpools or vortices. These whirlpools are clusters of compacted energy where virtual particles appear and disappear in the twinkling of an eye. These particles are called 'virtual' because they come and go so quickly. Virtual particles appear in pairs, a particle and its antiparticle. When they collide, they annihilate each other or self-destruct. All of the behaviors of virtual particles are due to their interactions with the chaotic sea of energy that we call empty space or the heavens. Infinite Energy creates and directs all of the behavior of the particle building blocks that compose everything.

How does a virtual particle become a real particle? Stephen Hawking postulates that virtual particle pairs born near black holes have a chance of becoming 'real' or physical matter. Like Pinocchio waiting for the Blue Fairy to become a real boy, if one of the two particles gets sucked into the black hole far enough to not be able to escape, the other one is free to live its life as a real particle. Without its anti-partner, it will not collide and self-destruct. NASA's Nuclear Spectroscopic Telescope Array (NuSTAR) watches the black hole at the center of our galaxy. When you realize that there is a black hole at the center of every galaxy, and that they spew jets of energy out of themselves in the form of light, heat and high-speed particles, you recognize how plausible this theory is.

Normal or real particles interact as well. Dr. Haisch and Dr. Rueda hypothesize that particles such as electrons, quarks and leptons, pick up energy, acceleration, and mass from being knocked around by the energy fields outside of them. The energy of mass and inertia is powered from outside the particles, not something that originates from the inside. Atomic particles dance about frantically, being pummeled around by the fields of space. Like being caught in a stormy ocean of energy, the atomic particles are being pushed and pulled in all directions by wave after wave. Dr. Haisch and Dr. Rueda believe all mass is due to the zero-point energy field. This is a creative field of what could be called the Holy Spirit.

The Bible tells us that everything is light and physicists agree. This light is not just what we can see, but includes the whole spectrum of energy. Photons and electrons are created both spontaneously and by stimulation. They are a bunching up of excitement in the electromagnetic field. I really had a difficult time imagining how electrons and photons just appear. One morning, my toaster started to burn bread and sent smoke throughout the room. I gazed at the swirling smoke in the light rays shining down through my skylights and realized that we see events in air all of the time, but if air isn't moving, changing or lacking, we don't notice them. If air starts to swirl and builds up enough velocity, the event is called a tornado, made from something we ordinarily don't even notice. Just like tornados in air, we only notice the infinite energy field when we see the particles, the particles that we perceive as matter.

Divine Light Fuels Our Temples

Photons fuel everything dealing with electromagnetic and weak fields, from photosynthesis to the chemical reactions inside animals, microbes, and us. When particles collide, they release light energy. This energy comes in particular sizes or packets. We call the energy packets of the electromagnetic field photons, but we know them as light particles. These energy packets come in certain sizes or particular amounts of energy, which are measured in quanta. Photons have no mass and that is why they move at the speed of light. Like a slinky or spring that can be compacted into a small circle or stretched to an undulating coil, light can act like a particle or a wave. They are rotating waves undulating through the universe carrying energy and information, and they power everything.

Electrons absorb photons like putting on super energy suits of certain sizes. Specific frequencies, or colors of suits work for some electrons and not for others. Electrons lose their energy in certain sized packets too. If an electron absorbs a large amount of energy it may leap free of its atom. Because electrons are negatively charged, if an electron jumps out of an atom, that atom becomes magnetically less negative or more positive. Like magnets, negatively charged electrons are attracted to the positively charged protons inside the atom's nucleus. Resembling dancers around a beautiful proton queen, the electrons stay on particular levels, only dancing where there is an empty space and only if no one is spinning the same way as they are. If you remember the little solar system-like drawings of the atom with the electron particle orbiting the nucleus toss the memory away, electrons blur across the atomic dance floor in an electron cloud, moving like waves not particles.

By absorbing enough photon light energy, a negatively charged electron can pull itself away from its positively charged nucleus. This leaves an empty space for another electron to be attracted to the nucleus. The remaining atom is called an ion because it is more positively charged after losing the electron. When this ion goes in search of an electron to partner with, it bumps along trying to pull off electrons and possibly destroying other molecules until it fills its electron quota. These types of collisions cause light to be emitted. Very sensitive photo-multiplying cameras like those used to see the stars can photograph this light.

Reactions inside our bodies cause photons, or light particles, to be emitted constantly. These light particles are called ultra weak photon emissions (UWPE). We are truly made of light. Additionally, the color of the light can indicate the status of our health. The colors of the emitted photons, which are in the visible light range between 200-400 nm, tell us whether the tissue is healthy or stressed. Blue is for healthy and red for diseased. The photographs measuring these emissions are made in very dark rooms that are guarded from exterior photons, in order to see and measure only the UWPE radiating from the subject. These photographs are proof that we are built and maintained with light energy.

We can measure the amount of this light (UWPE) emitting from other things as well, from test tubes and rocks, to fungi and animals. In fact, researchers must measure a test tube before they use it in an experiment, so they can subtract the tube's UWPE from the microbes' emission to calculate a true reading. Although photons are emitted during collisions and chemical bonding, sometimes they are also emitted spontaneously. Everything emits photons; it is only the rate and color of the emissions that vary. We are truly beings of light.

UWPE light is only as bright as a candle at a kilometer away. Though very weak, this light can stimulate healing. In 1923, Alexander Gurwitsch found that the root of one onion could increase cell growth in another even when the roots were separated by glass so that no sound, chemicals or touching was shared. The roots were visible to each other. The photons crossed the glass and directed the growth.

Additionally, these electromagnetic emissions can act as navigational tools, directing our cells where to go when we are being formed or when healing. Electromagnetic fields not only aid in cell growth but also direct where different types of cells migrate in order to organize tissues and organs. Basically, our DNA directs RNA to construct our amino acids and proteins that build our cells. Our epigenetic mechanisms turn on and off the DNA, instructing cells which genes to use and what kind of tissues they will differentiate to. Our electromagnetic field acts as a traffic cop, directing tissues to their correct positions in the structure of the organism.

This weak light is needed to heal and to produce healthy babies. Unfortunately, strong external electromagnetic fields can disrupt the cellular and structural growth of a fetus. These disruptions can cause lack of limbs, twisted bodies and stillbirths. Electromagnetic fields guide patterns of growth and structure in everything from one-celled creatures to multi-system organisms such as our bodies. It is written in Proverbs 20 verse 27, "The spirit of man is the candle of the LORD searching all the innermost parts of his being". The light that is generated by the infinite energy field penetrates and powers everything from electrons, atoms and molecules, to the cells, tissues and organs within our bodies. The electromagnetic field creates our building blocks, directs our growth and healing, and speeds all of our metabolic reactions. It is the light of life.

Our DNA is the reproductive organ of our cells. Up to 75% of all of our bodies' photon activity is located in our DNA. The photons in our DNA seem to be in rhythm together with the crests and troughs of their wavelengths peaking and dipping at the same time. This simultaneous rhythm is called coherence. Coherent light is what makes lasers so powerful. Lasers use excited combinations of elements whose magnet-like bonds hold photon energy. These bonds break apart, emitting light, which in turn tags other bonds to break up and emit light, and so on, all at the speed of light. Together, the coherent photons emit the powerful light of the laser. The bonds of our DNA emit synchronized, directional light much like a laser. Like each of our DNA is different, the light it emits is different, we each emit our own signature light frequency.

Amazingly, photons are not destroyed when they interact with electrons. They are absorbed and spit out over and over, and they move at the speed of light. They may be the reason we can see so quickly and carry on millions of reactions per cell per second. Light energy causes electrons to pop in and out of atoms enabling rapid chemical reactions. Scientists can watch the ultra weak photons being emitted depending on the amount of metabolic activity occurring. Our hands and faces emit more photons than the other places on our bodies. Luke 4, verse 40 carries an account of Jesus laying hands on people to heal diseases and Luke 1, verse 1; describes Jairus pleading with Jesus to lay hands on his daughter to heal her. Maybe this is why we lay our hands on people to heal them, like onion roots directing other root cells to divide and grow. More than ten times, the Bible refers to the shine of God's face, Jesus' face, and our faces. Whether it is restoring, bestowing favor, or in wisdom, the Bible tells us the light emitting from our faces is a great thing.

Light, born of the electromagnetic field, is the fuel that powers everything. Photons split water into oxygen and hydrogen ions, enabling plants, and some microorganisms, to grow and replenish our atmosphere. Through photosynthesis, they gather light, minerals and water to grow. Plants feed humans, animals, insects and some microbes. Light powers the fuel that develops into fossil fuels like oil, coal, and natural gases.

Most of our photons and oxygen are born from within our own sun. They also emerge from all of the stars that have ever existed. The infinite electromagnetic field creates them and us. We are temples constructed to hold the light and energy of the Divine. Light feeds us, energizes us, and enables us to interact with the environment around us.

Spirit Energy

We could not respond to the environment around us without photons and electrons to power our reactions. Photons fuel electrons. The exchanging of electrons is the mechanism that powers all of our senses. The receiving of external stimuli allows us to respond through our thoughts, emotions and actions. Electrons emit photons each time they drop down to lower energy levels. Absorbing photons excites electrons and raises their energy levels. Excited electrons contain the energy to fly out of their orbits to make and break bonds. But, where does all of the energy come from? Without this energy, electrons couldn't help atoms combine into molecules to create our cells, tissues and organs. With energy, electrons couldn't break molecular bonds. All of our cells need to break bonds to use glucose or sugar, and make the building blocks that maintain our bodies. Where does the energy to break bonds come from?

The energy of electrons and photons comes directly from the infinite energy field. Quantum physicists show us that electrons and photons are excitements that appear from the infinite energy field. An example of how this can happen is found in water. The importance of water has been known since the late 1940s when Albert Szent-Gyorgyi found two different states of water. One state that was normal and another state that contained excited electrons. Excited water electrons form into crystals and are energized directly from the infinite energy field.

In 1947, Albert Szent-Gyorgyi, the Hungarian born Nobel laureate that is called the father of biochemistry, wrote that the electromagnetic field excited, or energized, water molecules. Excited water is ready for electron transfer and normal water is not. This water wants to give away and gain electrons. Scientists know that the two kinds of water exist because they can measure a voltage at the interface between the two water states.

Excited water reduces the energy needed to break molecular bonds and helps the reactions in our bodies' to speed along. Normal water takes about the same amount of energy to exchange an electron as a soft X-ray. Can you imagine if every reaction in our bodies required the energy input of an X-ray? This amount of energy is not easily available in our bodies, but water is available to every cell.

Water is very important because it is the universal solvent. Almost everything dissolves in it. Since our bodies are over 70 percent water and every cell is hydrated inside and out, it makes sense that the bond breaking reactions in our molecules occurs with water. There is a problem though. The reactions require too much energy to break up molecules. Without excited electrons, our bodies' chemical reactions would require powerful acids and alkaline bases to build and maintain our cells. Although we use acids and alkaline bases to digest food in our stomachs and intestines, such powerful solvents would damage most of our other cells. Instead, infinite energy powers the reactions that build and maintain our bodies using excited water. Gyorgi explained that the electromagnetic field powers the electron exchanges by creating fluctuations that excite the electrons and generate photons. Electromagnetic photons excite the water in our bodies making the water easy to split. Gyorgi believed that the infinite energy field directly provided our bodies with the energy needed.

Excited water not only powers biochemical reactions, it is powering experimental cars and welding equipment. Job in chapter 38, verse 22, asked, "Have you seen the storehouses of the snow or seen the storehouse of the hail." Can we take this literally? Excited, crystallized water is a storehouse of energy. In order to explain water in crystal form during Job's lifetime, one would need to point to snow or ice. Today, we can use crystallographic x-rays to study the rings of linear water crystals and weights to measure the power they contain. Excited water is found in crystal rings that contain energy that comes from what physicists and engineers call zero-point energy or the energy that makes up the fabric of the universe.

Why is it important to be aware that we are directly powered by the energy of the universe? It is crucial to realizing that we are temples of energy. Realizing that the air we breathe, the water we drink, and the food we eat all appear due to the interactions of the infinite energy field, helps us to become conscious of what we are. Learning how the universe gives us the energy to live and the information to process enables us to transform our knowledge into an immoveable faith.

Strengthening our beliefs can transform our perceptions and our responses. We can do this by gaining new understanding and knowledge. Our perceptions shape our emotional and physical health. Becoming conscious, or mindful, to the interactions of infinite Spirit within our temples can transform our stress into faith. David told God in Psalm 59, verse 9; "O my strength, I will watch for you, O God, are my fortress". Watching for the Holy Spirit's interactions can become a continuous experience that strengthens our faith. Mindfulness of the Spirit energy within and without your body temple can free you from stress that leads to physical and emotional diseases.

Although the infinite energy field contains infinite amounts and frequencies of information, our temples are made to receive only certain types of signals or stimuli. Our bodies react to signals from our environments according to the size of the wavelength and the frequency of the information. Our bodies can only receive certain types of information, but if the signal is within narrow ranges, our bodies can decode the signals and react to it. If this wasn't true, we wouldn't need radios, televisions or cell phones to receive information.

All sensory information is energy waves. All information is energy! We receive information through our eyes, noses, mouths, skin, and tongues. Although other kinds of signals have been noted clinically to exist, information such as knowing when someone is watching hasn't been explored adequately enough to understand how we receive it. What scientists do know is our sense receptors receive information from our environment and use it to send electrical currents to the central nervous system (CNS). The CNS receives the messages, decodes them, and decides how to respond. Our beliefs dictate much of how our system responds.

Whether we are receiving the compression waves of touch, sound waves or light waves, our environment creates all of our sensory signals, and all energy waves start at the zero-point energy field or Spirit. The brain uses the energy produced from mechanical, chemical, or electrical stimulation, and combines it with the energy that each cell stores, to tell the body what to do, feel or think. Without the infinite energy field to send out information on, we would have nothing to respond to. There would be nothing to evoke memories, emotions and thoughts. Without interacting with the universe around us, we would have zero to live for. In Acts 17, verse 28, Paul told us "for in him we live and move and exist". We live, move, and exist in an infinite body of energy that enables us to feel, hear and see.

Every reaction inside of our bodies runs on light energy and electrons. Simply, this is how it works. The electrons are negatively charged and the protons inside the nucleus of an atom have a positive charge. Photons energize the electrons enabling them to jump out of the atom's orbit and break bonds. If an atom loses an electron, it then has more positive charge and is called a positive ion. Conversely, if an atom gains an extra electron, it is more negative and is called a negative ion. The more positively or negatively charged a molecule becomes, the stronger its magnetic pull. These magnetic forces make up the bonds that hold our molecules together. We use the transfer of electrons in our chemical reactions. We use excited electrons to split molecular bonds to run our bodies.

It is alien for us to think that at the smallest quantum level everything is really made of vibrating, rotating waves of the electromagnetic field. Normally, we picture electricity as electrons running from atom to atom creating an electron flow, which is called current. Many of us know that an insulator stops the flow of electricity. We think of an insulator as a substance that holds its electrons very, very tightly and doesn't like to gain or lose them. But, when speaking in terms of the infinite energy fields of the vacuum, electricity is measured by the frequency of the waves. A wavelength is the distance between the crests or the troughs, and the frequency of a wave is the number of the crests and troughs repeated per second.

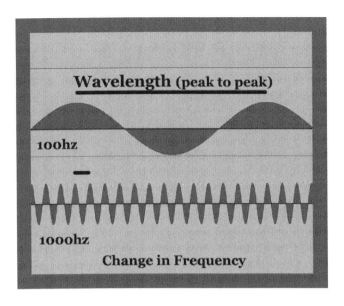

Wavelength (peak to peak)

100hz

1000hz

Change in Frequency

When we look at electrons at a very tiny level, as they interact with the electromagnetic energy field, electrons are standing waves that don't travel but merely undulate out and back in on themselves, like when you throw a stone into a kiddy pool. The ripples go out to the edge of the pool and return to the center over and over. These self-contained electron waves get attracted and repelled depending on the composition of the material around them. If the material has too large of gaps between its wavelengths (remember everything is energy waves), the electron can't move through it and the material is defined as an insulator. If the gaps between the wavelengths are small or overlapping, the electrons bounce through the material easily and the material is considered a good conductor. Scientists have replaced the picture of the electron particle orbiting around the atom with a picture of a swirling top bobbing placidly through an ocean of energy. The fabric of the universe dictates how the electron acts and an energized electron creates or destroys the bonds that hold the material world (and us) together. This is how Spirit or infinite energy holds the world together.

When looking at the bigger picture, our bodies use electricity in pretty much the same way that a simple circuit operates. Electrons and protons act like tiny magnets pushing and pulling everything into action. All we really need to know is positive and negative attractions hold together the bonds of our atoms; molecules are merely the partnering up of atoms, and molecules make up our cells' organelles. Electrons act like tiny magnets dancing between partners.

Every cell in our bodies stores potential energy like little batteries. This energy morphs into different forms such as electromagnetic, mechanical, and chemical energy. Our nerves and muscles use electrical currents to rapidly send messages. Our cells use it to make and reserve our energy in the form of adenosine triphosphate (ATP). From our sense receptors to our brains and back again, we use electricity to respond to our environment and transmit messages to the cells of our bodies. Electricity initiates secretion, excretion, movement, emotions, thoughts, and regulates and maintains homeostasis. Electromagnetic current fires our heartbeat and our brainwaves. We have electrical currents running up and down our nerve pathways telling us what we feel, hear, see, taste and touch, as well as where are body parts are located. Our neural receptors receive information in the forms of mechanical, chemical or electrical energy from our environment and convert it to electrical energy if necessary. Our brains and nervous systems process the information and redirect the energy to respond.

Operating together like miniature, electric train tracks, each neuron works by creating a magnet. With a positive charge on the outside of the cell, a negative charge on the inside, and an insulating wall or membrane in-between, neurons create a voltage or potential energy. Imagine each neuronal cell as a city with a wall around its entire circumference. The wall contains many gates. These gates are opened by many different keys, some pressure, some chemical, and some electrical. The wall of the city keeps small, positive people out while sequestering large, negative people inside the city against their wills. The more people in the crowded city, the harder it gets for others to get inside. The people on the inside become too crowded and are repulsed by people just like themselves that are trying to come in. This repulsion is called a concentration gradient and it leads to a high potential for something to occur. Just like a crowd that becomes agitated, when they reach a boiling point something is bound to happen.

The segregation of negative and positive people sets up a division or polarity between the positive people lining up against the wall on the outside and the negative people lining up against the inside. This polarity is called a membrane potential difference. So now we have crowding and conflict between people that are basically the same, concurrently with the forced segregation of different people causing the potential for something to happen!

Everyone is on edge waiting for a chance to get in or out of the city. They are excited! All they need is something to open and ease the escape through the wall. This opening is called a change in conductance. I once saw a concert crowd force a fence over when the gates were late opening. Everyone stormed the opening in the fence and the whole thing came down and everyone got in. Much like the concert crowd, when the correct gate pops open, the positive people flood in. If the crowd movement is large enough it causes a great earthquake to vibrate down the wall with the positive sodium ($Na+$) rushing in followed by the positive potassium ($K+$) running out to get away from the crowds. This raises the positive charge inside the cell above a threshold and causes even more gates to open along the adjacent wall. This is the firing of the neuron. The vibration doesn't stop at the first city but continues down the wall to the next adjoining city and the next and the next. When there are no direct connections, messengers called neurotransmitters jump motes or gaps between the cities, passing their messages to the receptors on the walls of the adjoining cities to open gates. Opening the gates of the next neuron city causes the storming of the next city walls and perpetuates the event. This is how our neurons send action potentials or signals to other neurons and enable our bodies to react.

We learn about the world though our sensory receptors. Our sensory receptor neurons use the energy from outside to send signals to our brains. Our brains redirect that same energy current to storm other gates, relaying commands back to the parts of our bodies that need to respond. Our sensory receptors are special cells that interact with the outside environment and send their messages up to our brains so that we can make judgments about our surroundings. They can warn us when we are in danger and need to act, and can initiate a number of interactions leading to responses in our body systems. These communications can even tell us which foods will make us sick, sometimes evoking a response so violent that it can cause gagging and vomiting immediately upon tasting or smelling. Smells can evoke memories, start salivation, turn on our digestive system, and be so sensitive that we subconsciously respond sexually. Our senses of vision, touch, smell, taste and hearing all instruct and inform us about how we need to respond to our environment using the energy started from outside of our bodies and created by the infinite field.

Touch

Relax and feel the air on your skin. We have tiny hairs that are attached to sensory neurons. What you are feeling is air pressure on the hairs pulling open the protein gates of your neurons with mechanical pressure, allowing the flow of ions through the cell membrane, and inducing an electrical impulse or spike. This ion flow fires afferent neurons, the type of neurons that send information in a spike up to the brain. The pressure that opens the gates of our touch sensors is a force, although we still don't know how every different type of sensory receptor is associated to different sensations. Our skin can detect temperature, pressure, pain and pleasure depending on such things as the intensity, duration, displacement, and frequency of the stimulus.

No one is ever really up against anyone or anything else. The repelling force between objects is what we sense as touch. All touch, whether a tickle or a punch, is really a force of the electromagnetic field. Touch is mechanical force that is transformed into electrical energy. Changing mechanical to electrical energy works like a windmill or waterwheel that turns a turbine to create energy. The mechanical energy of the air pressure is received by our neurons and incites the electrical energy that our central nervous system redirects to command our emotional and physical responses, and thoughts. We can react involuntarily with goose bumps caused by our erector pili muscles or we can think or perceive about the temperature of the wind and pull our sweaters closed. Emotionally, we may happily remember a warm fire or sadly recognize that our summer vacation is ending. Whether cold or hot, pain or pleasure, the most important ingredient is how we perceive or think about the energy signal of touch.

Position

Our brains know what positions our bodies are in all of the time. This is called proprioception meaning individual perception. Our muscle spindle receptors are like little springs that are pushed or pulled depending on the stretch of our muscles. The forces created by the push and pull tell our central nervous systems when the muscle contracts or lengthens. The soma, or body, of the neuron detects the position of our muscles and the rate of change in their length. Our muscle neurons are always turned on, only the rate of firing changes. A sustained firing of the neurons signals a maintained stretch. As the muscle stretch increases, muscle spindle fibers fire at a faster rate. The neuron soma receives input in short or long, and fast or slow current flows, and responds to the changes by changing the frequency of the constant spikes, much like a melody moving faster and slower, louder and softer. The magnitude or strength of the stimulus, determines the exact response. Once the response is sent down the axon of the neuron it is transmitted exactly, in an all or nothing spike. The brain receives this energy and redirects it by way of efferent neurons, which send commands to effectors like muscles and glands.

Interestingly, the sustained signals that maintain the tone of our muscles are constantly in a tug-of-war between straining and relaxing. If they weren't, we would either be frozen in position or in a heap of muscles and bones. Also, our neurons only react when the signals are strong enough otherwise, we would be responding to every little cell. Can you imagine being able to hear and respond to every one of the cells in our bodies? It is a good thing that the signals need to be loud and strong.

Hearing

The eardrum or tympanic membrane, acts like the head of a drum or a speaker cone. It vibrates with the compression waves that we call sound. Our drum moves at the same frequency as the sound waves, amplifies the waves, and then converts them into an ocean of rolling waves that capsizes our receptors. In our ears, hair cells called stereocilia are linked in rows at their tips. They sit in an ocean of potassium-rich extracellular fluid. Opposite the linked tips, the stereocilia create synaptic or messenger connections with both the sensory and the control or efferent neurons. Sound waves use air to vibrate the eardrum sending waves into a spiral channel called the cochlea. The snail-like cochlea funnels the waves further into the ear, where it pushes against the stereocilia causing the whole row to lie down, mechanically pulling open the gates. This allows the potassium ions to flow into the neural receptor, inducing an electrical spike down the wagging tail of the neuron to our brains. We are only sensitive to frequencies from around 20 to 20,000 cycles per second. We can receive only about 9 octaves because our sound wave receivers are tuned to those very limited frequencies. Cats and dogs can receive a range of 10.5 octaves.

Once the brain receives the energy from the sensory neuron and decodes it, the brain then sends a signal back to the efferent neuron, telling it to stiffen parts of the hair cells to listen for certain sounds. Conscience control of auditory sensitivity starts with fibers originating in the brainstem and they terminate on the inner hair cell of the ear. These fibers form what has been called the olivocochlear bundle. They spike in response to sound stimulation of the ear. Each fiber has a best frequency, which is the same frequency as the sensory neuron that it sits next to it on the hair cell. These fibers are thought to turn down ambient noise while allowing us to be responsive to important signals by stiffening the stereocilia. This is how we can listen for our children in a crowd of people or for any other specific noise in a noisy city.

Our sense of hearing is connected to our emotional responses and is so exacting that a recent study using functional magnetic resonance imaging found, while comparing the activation of women's brains in response to babies crying and other random noises, that certain emotional parts of their brains were stimulated only by the cry of the infant. Another study found that women, but not men, were awakened by the cry of their infant, even when sleeping heavily. This selective listening is sent from the ear, received in the brain stem, and controlled by hormones to activate the cerebral cortex. Our brain deciphers what we are hearing even in our sleep by receiving waves turning them into mechanical energy and back to electromagnetic energy. We can now really understand how living in a consistently noisy place can put extra pressure on our brains, and be detrimental to our health and our hearing, and how being quiet is so very important.

Smell and Taste

In our noses and mouths, chemical energy is changed into electrical energy. Each sensory neuron is reactive to just one type of odor or taste. The olfactory sensory neuron's cilia or nose hairs are projected into a gel or mucus and can only detect odors that are tiny aerosols and are dissolvable in water. We can detect up to 10,000 different scents. When specific odors are detected by means of G protein-linked receptors, chemicals are activated to open chemically unlocked gates and start the flow of ions, which activates the neuron and sends a nerve impulse that travels toward the sensory ganglion.

The olfactory bulb is part of the limbic or emotional brain connected by a huge number of inter-neuronal or neuron-to-neuron connections. The olfactory mechanism projects into the hippocampus, which is the part of the brain closely linked to memory and motivation. The hippocampal neurons may be why scents stimulate memories and can create cravings. Not only can we identify what each scent represents but scents can also embody memories and evoke emotions. The scents can bring back different memories depending on past imprinting. The smell of beer can represent the happy times at the college parties or the negative memory of one's father getting drunk over and over. A rose can remind one person of a loving note from a boyfriend and another of a sad funeral. We still don't know why the imprinting takes place but we do know that scents help with memory recall. Memories may be preserved by hanging acetyl and methyl groups on the histones and DNA in the hypothalamus cells of the brain due to sensory stimulations like emotions linked to smells.

The scents of certain phenolic aromatic, such as the smell of mint, from plants evoke specific emotions from us even if we have never smelled them before. Lavender and rose induce feelings of peace and calm, relieving stress. Most stress-relieving fragrances are strong enough to be measured physiologically utilizing heart rate, skin resistance, blood pressure, etc. Other odors such as tangerine elicit feelings of happiness and energy stimulation. Vanilla bean causes happy relaxed feelings. Some scents, such as ginger, decrease nausea and pain.

The effects of odors have even larger consequences. The odor you give off influences which people are attracted to you. Tests have suggested that red meat consumption has a negative impact on whether women find a man attractive. The body odor of non-meat eaters was found significantly more attractive and pleasant. The China Study, the largest dietary study ever done, found that the consumption of large amounts of meat and dairy products is associated with higher rates of cancer. We know that epigenetic changes can impede the factors that stop DNA point mutations, tumor growth and survival. Looking at animal studies, studies have found that when males have been epigenetically changed by administration of a toxin during gestation, females found them less attractive. These changes encouraged cancer in the epigenetically altered males and the altered odors of their pheromones were indicators of non-attractiveness and possibly disease or bad health to the females. Maybe human females can smell the poor health linked to over-consumption of domestic animals.

The Major Histocompatibility Complex (HCC) that women inherit from their fathers also affects women's noses and their choices in men. This complex is a set of molecules found on the outer membrane surfaces of our white blood cells. It identifies what is self and what is an invader and informs our immune system. In fact, HCC determines organ donor compatibility. We fight microbial invaders inside of our bodies by sniffing them out and destroying them with the macrophages of our immune system. If this mechanism gets confused, the results can be devastating to our health. This confusion is called an autoimmune disorder and causes our immune system to attack our own tissues.

Our noses can detect an odor from someone's HCC and recognize a person with a matching complex. Our body subtly sees the other person as part of our own bodies. Loving them is easy because subconsciously, we recognize them as one with our bodies. This is all linked to our immune systems. Biochemically, we love another when we recognize them as ourselves. This sounds a lot like the command to "love our neighbors as ourselves". We can see, and smell, others as one being with ourselves

Taste and smell are linked. If you have a stuffy nose, you most likely can't taste because much of the sensation that we call taste is actually smell. Taste utilizes chemical energy. Our taste sensory receptors project microvilli hairs into a pore or small hole. There are many sensory receptor cells in each bud. The specific types of receptors send the signals of the particular taste to the nerve. Different regions of the tongue contain different types of taste buds or gustatory papillae. Different people have dissimilar amounts of taste buds causing some people to be very sensitive, while others can't decipher much. Specific types of tastes, such as salty, sour, sweet, or bitter are induced by the increase or decrease of certain substances. For instance our table salt (NaCl), the mineral, sodium tastes salty. Sour is characterized by increased hydrogen (H+) or acid (pH), so what we taste as sour is acidic like the citric acid in lemons.

Sweet, bitter, and what is called the fifth taste, umami or the taste of protein, can block potassium channels, and stimulate a neuropeptide named G protein and other chemicals, thus activating both chemical and electrical energy. This allows ions (like Ca++ or Cl-) to flow and release messengers, which induce electric spikes. It has been hypothesized that at least five different mechanisms are in place to sense bitter tastes. Bitter is very important because it can be the signal to keep us from eating poisonous or harmful bitter substances. These bitters include some alkaloids in plants. Scientists believe that gustducin (G protein) may also be a safeguard in the stomach by stimulating vomiting in the presence of hazardous substances. Chemical energy and electrical energy is used to detect what we think of as smell and taste. Energy is all that exists to sense or perceive! We taste and smell nothing but infinite energy.

Our sense of taste and smell are initially experienced in the womb as the flavor of the amniotic fluid. What your mother ate, drank and smoked still affects what you find appealing. The experiences from our mothers continue in the breast milk if we were nursed. What we find enjoyable to eat are colored by these experiences and determine our flavor preferences. We learn odors and tastes while we are in the uterus from what our mothers' enjoy. Odors also become paired with emotions depending on the emotions we are feeling when the odors are first encountered. Odors and emotions can be linked and we can learn to like or dislike foods that are linked to the odors. One example is the scent of mint, which can remind us of candy or medicine depending on our first experience with it.

Sight

Have you wondered why we see a thing as solid objects if everything is mostly empty space? Lets examine say an apple. Apples that are red absorb most of the light waves that are in the frequency of green and reflect the rest out. The photosynthetic cells within our eyes absorb the light waves that reflect off of the apple. The light waves we absorb from the reflection react by sending messages to our optic nerve and our brain constructs a form inside our minds much like a computer constructs a three dimensional model from data we give it. Like our muscles, our eyes are always turned on. For our vision, we use solar energy or photons to generate chemical energy, which produces electrical energy to fire our neurons. Our eyes are photosynthetic! Our vision works opposite our other senses because our retinal sensor's membrane gates stay open in the dark and closed when they receive light. Scientists think this is one of the reasons we can see so quickly.

When photons hit the visual receptors in our eyes, their membranes' pigments absorb the light. The light activates a pigment called rhodopsin in our rods. Rhodopsin, known as visual purple, is responsible for the first events leading to the perception of light with our eyes. It is a protein receptor sitting on the membrane of our rods. Rods are the light and dark receivers that enable us to see in the dark.

A photon is absorbed causing the receptor in the rod's membrane to change shape to form a key. This key, together with the G protein, is able to unlock the energy of chemical bonds. This energy signals the closure of the ion gates. Closing the gates stop the neurons from firing and inhibit the neurotransmitters from jumping the gaps. Because these neurotransmitters inhibit the optical receiving neurons from firing, stopping them excites a current from the receiving neurons through to the optical nerve to the brain.

Inside our eyes, light acts as photon energy, exciting bonds to shape shift. This shift induces the release of chemical energy, which closes the ion gates and stops the release of inhibiting messenger neurotransmitters. When the inhibiting neurotransmitters no longer reach the receiving neurons, the neurons fire electromagnetic energy to send a current to the brain. In this way, our eyes are pretty much always turned on and ready to receive energy with a huge amount of receiving sensors called rods and cones.

Different wavelengths activate different rods and cones in different part of the retina. Our brains receive the input and must decipher it. We construct a model inside our minds of what we perceive on the outside, which of course, is mostly empty space. The energetic currents of our sight receptors are constantly turned on and ready to receive the energy of a photon reflecting off objects. Objects, which are merely waves interacting with an ocean of energy waves, absorb certain wavelengths and reflect others. Our visual receptors stand ready to receive and send the information to our brains to construct an internal sculpture of the world around us. This is a sculpture that is individual to each of us. It is our minds' perception of what exists on the outside. The things that we perceive are really only interactions of wave patterns and not solid objects. We paint the reflections of different wavelengths of energy inside of our mind's eye.

Sound waves, molecules, ions, photons, pressure, stretching, and temperature all cause electrical currents to run through our neurons towards the brain. In this way, the universe around us constantly interacts with our neurons to create impulses, which our brains detect and decode to control our bodies. We redirect the energy around us that bumps into our skin, ears, eyes, nose, and mouths to tell our neurons what to do. Receptors also fire our emotional center and thought processes. Our thoughts direct the energy from external stimuli for use inside the body. Without the infinite energy to receive and react to, there would be nothing to sense, nothing to taste, smell, touch, see or think about. Descartes' famous quote; "I think, therefore I am" is in realty; I interact, therefore I think.

Faith Energy

The Bible tells us that if we have faith we can move mountain and stop storms. It is intriguing to contemplate the idea that our thoughts and emotions may affect the energy outside of our bodies. We have focused our thoughts to direct energy inside our bodies since before we were born. Our emotions cause internal changes without even trying. If we practice directing energy on the outside with the same focus and intensity, could we redirect energy outside with the same effectiveness? Our nervous system is made up of billions of separate neurons that receive electrical signals from external stimuli and other neurons. These neurons generate energy signals of their own that are sent to more neurons. In just the brain, we have about 10 billion neurons, each with about 10,000 connections all firing with electromagnetic energy. That is a lot of energy to direct.

The idea of our thoughts, emotions and prayers being measurable outside of our body seems improbable, but using magnetoencephalography, we can measure the energy of the brain without touching or attaching anything directly to our heads. Magnetoencephalography (MEG) is a technique used to map cognitive brain processes and functions in the brain. It takes approximately 50,000 neurons firing together to create a measurable output for a Magnetoencephalogram or electroencephalogram. The MEG (and EEG) signals are derived from the sum of ionic currents flowing through the membranes of neurons during the firing of neurons. This is the flow of ions like $Na+$ or $K+$ across the membranes of the neurons. In short, the firing of many, many neurons is measured. In Hungary, scientists measured over 12,000 dendrites or hairs on a single pyramidal neuron in the hippocampus of our brain. Pyramidal neurons, the primary excitatory units in our brains, may receive up to 30,000 excitatory inputs and 1700 inhibitory inputs. That means our neurons are incredibly interconnected enabling them to communicate and integrate continuously. Scientists can measure the brain without touching our bodies by picking up the energy that is transmitted while it jumps from neuron to neuron. This proves that the energy of our brain is measurable outside the body.

The electromagnetic energy of our hearts is more powerful than our brains. Our thoughts and emotions command electromagnetic energy that interacts with the energy fields outside of our bodies. Jesus said in Mark 11, verse 23, Matthew 17, verse 20 and chapter 21, verse 21, that it is possible to move mountains with a spoken command and faith. In Mark chapter 9, verse 23, Jesus said, "Everything is possible for him who believes." Scientists can measure the energy our brains and hearts put out into the universe through our thoughts and emotions. Could this be the energy employed to move mountains?

Over and over in the Bible, we are told that Spirit gives us life. Where is the proof that Spirit breathes life into us? One thing scientists can't yet explain is how the neurons in the brain start to fire for the first time. The scientists that have studied fetal chickens from their first cells until birth, believe they have found the place in the brain that first fires with energy. A current spontaneously starts a wave across the brain once the cells have differentiated enough. Is this when the Breath of God enters our body temples?

When the cells first start out they are all the same, parts of the sperm and the ovum. They start dividing and they begin to change into different tissue depending on the epigenetic tags on their chromatin. Epigenetic mechanisms turn on and off specific genes to tell cells their location and the job they will do for the body. Once they have differentiated enough to do their job, an energy wave washes through the brain suddenly for the first time. The energy starts at one point and spreads out like a wave over the brain. Is this spontaneous wave of energy what is described in Genesis 2, verse 7 as "the breath of life" or in Ecclesiastes 12, verse 7 as the Spirit of God that returns to him when we die? This energy animates our bodies. It emits electromagnetic waves and ultra weak photons of light that can be measured outside of the body.

But, this is not the only place Spirit Energy touches. In much the same way as the brain, an energy wave spontaneously begins the beating of our hearts when the cells have differentiated and built our cardiac tissue. In II Corinthians 4, verse 6, Paul said, "For the God who said, Let there be light in the darkness, has made this light shine in our hearts so we could know the glory of God that is seen in the face of Jesus Christ." Our hearts beat due to electrical pulses running through nodes and specialized cells. Our heart is merely a hollow muscle that is the size of our fist. It has two upper chambers that get blood from the body and lungs and two lower chambers that pump the blood to the body and the lungs. Without an electrical spark to jump-start our muscle we couldn't get oxygen to our bodies. The electrical impulse races from the sinus node through the upper chambers or atria, causing them to squeeze blood into the lower chambers called the ventricles. When the electrical charge reaches the atrioventricular node in the middle of the heart it pauses and then races throughout the lower chambers sending blood throughout the body. Then the spark starts back at the beginning. The PBS show called NOVA tells us that the average heart beats 100,000 times per day and 35 million times in an average lifetime. If the electricity stops, we either need a pacemaker or a grave.

The heart, if it is beating properly, has well-coordinated electrical activity. The heart has over 40,000 neurons that not only cause it to beat but also communicates with the brain via the vagus nerve and the spinal cord. This energy can easily be measured outside of the body by instruments that pick up electromagnetic fields. One such instrument is a superconducting quantum interference device, which gives us magnetocardiograms. The heart's magnetic field is more than 1000 times more powerful than the brain's magnetic field. Just like light, these electromagnetic fields interact with the other fields close to them, but how they affect each other is not yet understood. We manufacture these fields all of the time. When a body or a cell has no energy it is dead. Electromagnetic energy runs the lights in our homes and it makes our hearts beat and our brains fire. We are truly the lights of the world.

Albert Einstein told us "all matter is energy". Energy is exchanged all of the time on many levels. There are over 100 billion neurons in our bodies firing bits of electromagnetic energy in order to communicate, move, think and feel. Sometimes called spirit, chi or vitality, electromagnetic energy moves up and down our bodies. We perceive it often without realizing. We feel joyful and free after forgiving someone or doing a good deed. We feel the vigor that sweeps over us when we are doing something we really love. If we are aware of this spirit flow, we can direct it to help us heal or be energized. Prayer, meditation, and chanting (repeating any word like Jesus or thank you), all increase the flow of Spirit energy. Ephesians 5, verses 8-10, instructed us to "walk as children of the light". Learn to use the energy that you have been given.

When we speak of energy flowing through the body, you may think that we are speaking of an ethereal hocus pocus that can't be measured. This isn't true! The body's autonomic nervous system (the system that runs the things we don't think about like sweating, digesting, etc.) has two branches that work at odds with each other. The sympathetic side fires the nerves, which begin the fight or flight mechanisms and the parasympathetic side fires the rest and restore systems. What we believe controls how we perceive and how we react to external and even internal or imagined stimuli. Beliefs tell the emotional brain which side to excite. If we react in fear, worry, and anxiety, our emotional brains tell the sympathetic system to steal the energy from our digestion, immunity, elimination, and many other tissues in our bodies. If we trust, we send energy to the systems that repair and restore our bodies.

Our fears are learned. Scientists tell us that most people are born with just two fears, a fear of falling and a fear of intense stimuli such as loud noises. Most other fears are adaptations to protect us from our environment. Some fears can be inherited through epigenetic mechanisms. Fear is a great way to learn to premeditate real and immediate danger in order to survive, but it can be wired into our brains to cause stress, worry, anxiety and depression. We can make the choice to react with trust or react with fear. If we remember that past memories and experiences construct our egos and that future worries are extensions of those egos, we can decide to live each moment in trust and faith.

We make choices that control how we use our energy every day. 1 Thessalonians 5, verse 16 tells us, "Be joyful always". It gives us energy! Have you ever worked really hard at something, and felt not tired, but exhilarated at the end of the day? I worked at building and painting new kitchen walls and after eight coats of paint, I got the color right. I felt like I had really accomplished something and now every time I see my kitchen, I admire the color. It makes me feel good. Feeling good, accomplished, and joyous is what builds and conserves energy. I could have become frustrated and angry that the color wasn't right after the first couple of paint coats and given up but then I would have felt bad and given my energy up to negative thoughts. That is wasteful! The Divine gives us energy each day to go through life. How we conserve or waste that energy is up to each of us.

Past regrets, anger, hate, and sadness are expensive. It wastes our energy and no one gains from it. Whether or not you voice your anger, frustration, or hate, no one gets the benefit of the energy and no one feels better because of it. It is just gone. If you continue to feel these negative feelings, it costs you, not the person or persons that you are not forgiving. Its giving energy to a situation that is gone. It is like feeding the dead. That is not to say that we will never be sad or angry or frustrated, only that continued feeding of the past costs us too much of the power that is given to us. Continued dwelling on past negative emotions and holding on to negative attitudes drain our power and can lead to depression and inflammation. Chronic negative emotions and stress can cause chronic inflammation, which is a leading cause of disease. It is time to take back the vitality that is promised to us.

We have been given light or Spirit Energy but how we use it is up to us. The universe gives us the energy, how we use it to perceive the world through our senses and mind is up to us. Spirit gives us the energy to move and to do the things that we want. It is up to us to shine this light brightly and positively in the world.

Be ye Transformed by the Renewing of Your Mind

Energy, in the forms of electricity and magnetism, is used by our bodies to bring information to our brains about our environment. It is used to direct our muscles, organs, tissues and chemicals. But, how do our thoughts and emotions fit in? Amazingly, scientists have found that our brains are not static but instead they are always transforming. In Romans 12, verse 2, the Bible told us, "and be not conformed to this world: but be ye transformed by the renewing of your mind, that ye may prove what is that good, and acceptable, and perfect, will of God". Our brains are not stuck. We can renew neurons, alter brain structure and transform the epigenetic mechanisms. These changes enable us to live healthy and happy lives. Our brains are constantly generating new neurons in response to our changing environment, emotions, stress levels and physical activities. Doctors can no longer tell us that something is just in our heads because if it's in our minds it can change the health of our physical bodies.

In addition to making new neurons, our brains are literally able to change our bodies at the level of how our genes are interpreted to make amino acids and proteins. The study of these changes is called epigenetics. This is where following the Bible's directions for how to live gets exciting. We can transform how we construct the building blocks of our bodies by changing how we feel, what we do, what we eat, and how we take care of our environment. Deep prayer and meditation changes how we copy our DNA. Music changes it. Love changes it. Most importantly, what we believe, and how we perceive the world around us changes how we copy our genes.

How we perceive and respond to external and internal inputs alters how our DNA is used to make the RNA (Ribonucleic acid). RNA constructs the amino acids used for peptides, proteins, enzymes, and other things our bodies need to maintain health. We can start generating new neurons, increase gray matter, and initiate more connections between existing neurons! We have ways to renew our minds! What we do, say, feel, and think affects the way our genes are expressed. In other words, what we think affects what we feel and do, and these feelings and actions can dictate how our DNA is copied. Epigenetic regulation of genes not only affects our cells and bodies, but also those of our children and grandchildren. We have in our hearts and minds, the ability to change the way our DNA is expressed for evolutionary change. Things like falling in love, exercise, praying, music, and learning something new can tell the body to copy a different part of a gene. Conversely, stress and depression can also affect whether or not a gene is expressed or copied. Making these very small changes can lead to the construction of a different species of protein. Epigenetic changes can turn on genes so they can be copied and conversely it can turn them off. These small differences in protein factors can mean the difference between depression and contentment, or between a healthy, resilient cell that can withstand environmental assaults and a rogue cell that can become cancer. We can transform our minds and bodies by how we perceive, believe and act!

DNA gives the directions on how to build all of the components our bodies need to run but doesn't really give us the ability to adapt. After mapping all of our genes, scientists were surprised how few coding genes we had (they threw out the non-coding genes as junk!). Coding genes are the ones that tell our RNA how to make amino acids. The number of genes didn't add up to the amount of different peptides, proteins, and other things our bodies use constantly. Other than transposons, which are codes that jump in and out of our DNA, scientists didn't know how to manipulate the genome to receive enough directions to construct all the parts we need. Epigenetic mechanisms give us the ability to adapt. Epigenetics explain how the DNA is altered and copied to get the number of protein variations found within our bodies. The epigenetic mechanisms work by adding punctuation to the language of our DNA. As we know, by adding and deleting punctuation, we can change where a sentence or a word starts and stops, how it is read, and its meaning. This is how epigenetic tags change the way our genetic code is translated. A methyl group hung in our DNA, or an acetyl group attached to a DNA protein called a histone, tells us where to start or stop copying and whether to make part of a gene or not.

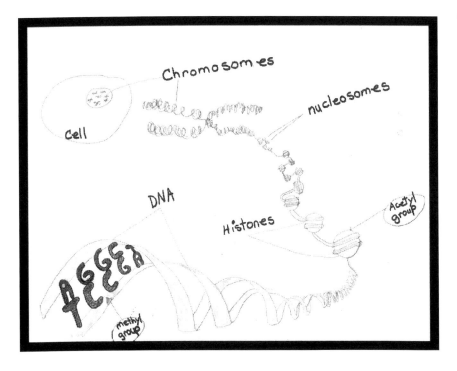

Our genes are found in the actively copied regions of our DNA. The familiar double helix or DNA ladder is wrapped around 8 specialized proteins called histones. How tightly the DNA is wrapped around the histones dictates whether an area gets copied. The tightness or looseness is dependant on whether the magnetic bonds and folding allow enough room for the copying equipment to do their work. Different groups attached to the histones or the DNA dictate whether the enzymes and factors can reach the areas marked to start copying. These marked areas are called promoters. The DNA copy-ability is changed by how many added groups are hung either directly on certain parts of the DNA backbone or on the histones' tails. They can also be hung directly on the RNA to stop the construction of amino acids.

Once again electrons, or their lack, dictate the strength of the bonds holding the added groups. Thankfully, there are enzymes that can remove or add these groups and bring our genetic code back to building the things we need. We can reset or reboot our immunity and other factors. The Bible shares ways to do it. Until now, it was not understood how the Biblical instructions worked to heal our bodies and minds.

Too Much Information

To understand how epigenetic renovation works and what we can do to enhance the transforming of our minds, we need a simple understanding of how the amino acids, peptides, and proteins are made and how they affect the central nervous system. Why is this so important? Bruce Lipton, a developmental biologist, realized that our genome was half DNA and half proteins. He further recognized that proteins, in forms of receptors and channels, respond to external stimulus causing changes in the way our genome was made into RNA and then into amino acids.

Amino acids are the building blocks of the peptides, polypeptides, proteins, and other factors that transform our brains. Peptides and proteins have many important jobs in our bodies from enzymes that help to speed up the making of our energy (ATP), to the gates and channels that open and close to fire our neurons when we receive sensory information. To make our proteins, we use only twenty-one standard amino acids, which are found in all animals whether single-celled or human. Nine of these amino acids are considered essential, which means we don't make them and must get them from what we eat. We get them from legumes, seeds and nuts, as well as leafy greens and animals.

Amino acids are made from the same elements we find everywhere. Carbon, oxygen, hydrogen, and nitrogen are the ones we find a majority of the time. Amino acids consist of a chain of carbon atoms with a side chain that is different for each amino acid. Some amino acids have negative charges and some have positive charges. Some are uncharged but polar, with one side negative and one side positive. Polar amino acids love water (hydrophilic). Some are uncharged, non-polar and hate water (hydrophobic). Polar means that they share their electrons unevenly. The negatively charged electrons spend more time with one part of the molecule making it something of a magnet for positively charged molecules. All of these diverse electromagnetic charges explain how the amino acids parts fit together with different kinds of linkages or bonds, positive to negative, hydrophobic to lipids (fats), hydrophilic to sugars, etcetera. This may seem like too much information, but it explains how the infinite energy field, through electrons and negative and positive charges, interacts with our every building block and every reaction. Without Divine Energy, nothing would hold together to construct or maintain our building blocks, our cells, or our bodies.

These charges are very important in how the finished proteins are folded as well. The way proteins fold forms their shape. Their shape designates how they fit with other molecules to do their jobs. We see this in how our neurotransmitters fit with their receptors in the gaps (synapses) between our neurons and the lock and key formations of our membrane gates. Folding is so important that misfolded membrane proteins have been linked to the plaques that cause Alzheimer's. Unfolding a protein can denature it and render it useless.

Our peptides and proteins are built of amino acids from the recipes found in our genetic code. Short chains of amino acids are called peptides, the medium ones are polypeptides, and the longer ones are called proteins. The peptides used by our neurons are called neuropeptides. These peptides transform depending on our emotions, stress level, social interactions, learning situations, and environmental changes. They translate what we feel, sense, and learn into changes in our physical bodies. Emotional and physical inputs tell our bodies how and when to make our peptides.

Neuropeptides are signaling molecules and they turn up or down (modulate) the activities or lack of activities of our brains. They switch on and off functions like analgesia (pain killing), appetite or lack of, reward behavior, learning, and memory. Neuropeptides enable our neurons and as such, our brains and bodies to be dynamic, transforming, and adapting to our surroundings. They adapt because our DNA can't. Neuropeptides are constructed to communicate with receptors that fit with them exactly to excite or inhibit actions in our neuron receptor cells.

Because depression is so prevalent, we hear a lot about neurotransmitters like serotonin and dopamine. The difference between neurotransmitters and neuropeptides is that neurotransmitters usually affect the energy spikes that excite neurons to send messages to and from the brain, muscles and sensory receptors. Neuropeptides have many jobs, sometimes with actions that may be active for long periods. They can affect behavior, emotions, as well as hormones. Often, neuropeptides co-exist with neurotransmitters at the synaptic gaps, as well as in the soma, dendrites and other places in the neuron. Examples of neurotransmitters are: norepinephrine, GABA, acetylcholine, dopamine, adrenaline, glutamate, and serotonin. Examples of neuropeptides or peptide hormones are oxytocin (activated when you fall in love or have a baby), vasopressin (balances water and salts, and affects blood pressure), and endorphins (activates opium-like receptors to dull pain and lift mood).

Specific activities trigger chemical factors that cause changes in the central nervous system. It is believed that this is how we adapt to our environments, learn and remember. One example of a factor that transforms our brains due to emotional and environmental changes is called brain derived neurotrophic factor or BDNF. BDNF is a protein that stops programmed neuron death and tells baby cells to form new neurons. Our experiences stimulate biochemical factors like BDNF to modify the structure of our nervous system. Our physical bodies transform due to changes in what we do and perceive. This remodeling includes changes to our existing neurons and synapses by: the thickening of axons. This increases the speed of neural firing by increasing the number of dendrites and spines to enhance the number of connections each neuron has. This speeds up our responses and processes making it easier to learn and remember.

Serotonin, nitric oxide, glucose and corticoids (stress hormones) are some of the substances that control the level of BDNF in our brains. These are some of the things that can be controlled by following the directions we are given in the Bible. We can raise our BDNF with increased physical activity, enriching our environment, and trying new things. Most importantly, BDNF reacts to our responses to the things that go on around and to us. *What we believe is happening is*

more important than what is really going on. In other words, if you think a person loves you or hates you, whether or not they do or don't isn't important to your peptides. Only what you think, feel, say, and do are important. If you believe something is scary, your peptides will respond with fear and release adrenaline and cortisol. This throws your body into fight or flight mode, and stops immunity and digestion among other things. If you believe that you love someone, your body responses with oxytocin, which builds feelings of bonding, pleasure, and good mood. In John chapter 14, verse 12, Jesus said that believing allows us to do greater things than he did, and in verse 14, Jesus told us that he *will* do anything that we ask in his name. Our beliefs are powerful. They can transform the structure of our brains and the stress level in our bodies.

This is how BDNF transforms; the gene for BDNF permits four different ways to read the recipe (transcriptions) with two different sites for each. This allows many slight differences depending on type and location of the neural activity that triggers the copying of the gene. What this means is, the way the gene is copied to manufacture BDNF depends on what turns on the process. Our emotional responses and physical activities determine the amount and the way the factor is made. This is how our nervous system reacts to different mental and physical stimuli.

Why is increasing our BDNF important? Research has linked low BDNF to depression. Depression lowers immunity, slows healing, and impairments memory and brain function. It is also central to enhancing brain transformation to help us continue to adapt to our environment and the stressors that bombard us daily. Enhancing our environments can help our brains to generate new cell growth, repair injuries, and produce the factors that keep us healthy. The Bible has given simple instructions that enhance our environment and behaviors to transform our minds, improving mood, health and longevity.

Changes we make enable us to renew our minds and shape our whole being. Ephesians 4, verse 23 told us "to be made new in the attitude of your minds".

Sing unto the Heavens with a New Song

In Psalm 150, verses 3-6, David instructed us to "Praise him with trumpet sound; praise him with lute and harp! Praise him with tambourine and dance; praise him with strings and pipe! Praise him with sounding cymbals; praise him with loud clashing cymbals!" Whether by singing, dancing, or banging a tambourine to the beat, music changes our brains! Each of the things listed in this verse can re-wire the structure of our brains and how our neurons fire. Singing, dancing and playing musical instruments all enhance the way our bodies react and use music to improve our lives. The brain and body react differently to different types of music. The correct styles of music can increase positive emotions, improve memory, and aid in creating lasting relationships. Just listening to music can change our moods and boost our health.

Music is great for our bodies and minds. It can change our moods and get us up to our feet to exercise. David in Psalm 149 verse 3 said, "Let them praise his name in the dance: let them sing praises to him with the tambourine and harp". Singing, playing a musical instrument, or dancing to music connects the hindbrain to the forebrain and midbrain. This happens because our emotional, motor, and auditory systems are connected when we listen to music. We receive music with our auditory system. Our auditory system then causes neurons to fire in the motor cortex of our brains. This is why we tap our feet, sway, clap, and dance to the music.

When you sing and dance, or play a musical instrument, you cause positive reorganizational changes in your brain's thinking cap or cortex. These changes increase your abilities to think, reason, balance, and coordinate. But cortical reorganization is plastic, which means it can change back if you stop singing and dancing. So consistently singing, dancing and playing instruments, for as little as twenty minutes a day, can help to fine-tune and heal our brains.

Music increases the thickness of our brains. Studies using positron emission tomography (PET) and functional magnetic resonance imagery (FMRI) have shown that musical training enhances the density of our gray matter. Gray matter is comprised of mostly neuronal cell bodies, dendrites, and capillaries. Music also enhances the structure of our white matter bundles, which are mostly mylinated neuronal axons of the motor circuits in the brain. Music causes these neuroplastic (malleable neuron) changes throughout the whole nervous system. Although, musical training before the age of ten or twelve may elevate these changes even further, musical practice can induce new neuron growth in people of all ages. These re-organizational changes improve not only auditory and motor skills, but also enhance our executive functions to help us learn, make good decisions, and improve memory.

Practicing music improves memory and motor skills. Tests have shown that the density of the hippocampus, or memory center, was greater in musicians than non-musicians. Information transfer between hemispheres of the brain was also enhanced. Musical practice used to synchronize or entrain our brains to the beat, can improve the motor control of Parkinson's and stroke patients. Just twenty minutes a day of piano and drum training can increase the speed and precision of body movements and cause lasting improvements in sensory-motor integration.

Watching brain wave patterns have proven that listening to music can even benefit the brain of a coma patient. Musical training, especially if started young, enhances the overall plasticity, or adaptability, of the brain and enhances many kinds of learning. Denser gray matter, and increased neurons and dendrite connections act like wider freeways. They give us additional, faster pathways to deliver messages that help us to move, learn, remember, and control our emotions. Long-term musical training thickens the corpus callosum, or bridge that lies between the two sides or hemispheres of the brain increasing the connections between them. Music can start the flow of stored memories and thoughts across the corpus callosum. It can synchronize both sides of our brains, helping both sides to work in harmony. When both sides of our brains work in tandem, we have increased physiological, emotional and cognitive functioning. We think and feel better! It is important in controlling our moods and social interactions. The National Institutes of Health reported in October of 2011 that extreme cases of stunted connections between the hemispheres result in autistic affects such as excessive fear in new situations and failure to play with others. Further, this stunting has been linked to use of antidepressants during pregnancy. Musical training can facilitate new neural growth and helps reconnect both sides of the brain. Reconnecting hemispheres with musical training elevates our moods, aids in social development, and alleviates depression. It enhances the functioning of our bodies and minds.

Learning music, whether singing, dancing or playing, bundles our nerve pathways and builds new ultra-fast nerve freeways. Musical training affects the speed and rhythm of the firing of neuron systems that work together. These firing networks create systematic wave patterns or brain rhythms. Electroencephalographs (EEGs) measure them and we know them as the beta, theta, alpha, gamma, and delta states in our brains. Changing the pattern of oscillation in the brain enhances learning and performance. When we develop musical expertise, we improve our long-term memory processes and cause structural and functional rewiring in our hippocampus or memory center. Since music can influence the functioning of the hippocampus, it is believed that music training causes an epigenetic boost in neurogenesis in the hippocampus. The births of new neurons can help patients with depression and anxiety. Drumming circles and positive, emotion-evoking music can elevate mood and reduce stress.

Music causes new neurons to grow in our brains! Music significantly increases the births of new neurons by enhancing a factor called brain derived neurotrophic factor (BDNF). BDFN promotes the birth of new neurons and new synaptic connections between brain neurons. This is a key to good brain health. It also reinforces and expands behavioral or habitual memory, which is the type of memory that can be degraded as we age. Musical training can protect the aging brain from a cognitive decay. Sustained musical exposure and training protects our brains from degrading as well as the new epigenetic drug treatments.

Though music is merely patterns of sound waves, it affects our emotions and creates moods. We all know that the right music can create a romantic dinner or energize exercise participants at a fitness center. It all depends on the dynamics of the tune. Some music creates a desire to move and energizes us. Music also helps us to relax and learn. Music is so powerful, it can pull us back to the memory of what we were experiencing when we first heard a song, complete with sounds, colors, who we were with, and even what we ate. Couples share their own songs that draw them closer by evoking a shared memory.

People everywhere respond emotionally and physically to music stimuli, but we only share the amazing ability to enjoy music with very few creatures on earth. Have you ever wondered why music can do this to us? It begins when music is received by pressure receptors in our ears, but unlike other noises, musical dynamics are assessed and sent to our emotional brain. Music activates several parts of our emotional brain, as well as our motor and visual cortices.

Music integrates and engages the forebrain, midbrain, and hindbrain to give our bodies the ability to enjoy the emotions, memories, and movements that are connected to music. And, these things can happen with or without lyrics.

Music enters and affects the brain when the ears hairs and bones receive external sound pressure waves. The waves of music fire neurons to transfer the information to the temporal lobes near our ears. Besides receiving music, the temporal lobes also play a vital role in forming and retrieving memories, and help to integrate our memories with sensations of taste, sound, sight, and touch. This may be the reason why a song can bring on such vivid memory playbacks. The temporal lobes then transfer the information about music using the energy of neuron firing to activate the other parts of the brain.

The musical information then engages the hypothalamus. The hypothalamus regulates your levels of pain, pleasure, emotional response, and sexual satisfaction, as well as hunger and thirst. It also regulates pulse, blood pressure and breathing. It receives information about how full you are, whether it is light or dark, how warm your skin is. It tells us whether to vomit in the presence of a toxin or if something smells good enough to eat. It modulates the food you eat. One study called 'The lighter side of music' demonstrated how music could adjust our appetite and help us to lose weight, helping us to realize the importance of the correct music at a meal. The music you listen to at dinner affects your digestion. The right type of music calms our emotional brain and modulates our eating behaviors.

The hypothalamus is also part of the hypothalamus-pituitary-adrenal axis, which regulates our fight or flight mechanisms and stress hormones. It influences anxiety and depression. The old idiom 'music soothes the savage beast' is true! Music can soothe the beast in all of us by calming our emotional brain and lowering our stress hormones.

Scientists have demonstrated that exposure to pleasurable music for as little as 21 days significantly increased the BDNF found in the hypothalamus, and aids in the growth of new neurons and brain plasticity. By increasing BDNF, music can have positive affects on blood pressure, cardiac heartbeat, respiration, and emotional states. BDNF is involved in the growth, survival, maturation and function of neurons in our central nervous system. Music, by increasing this factor, helps us to rewire our brains. It enhances the way we function in life by relieving depression, anxiety, and other mood disorders. It uplifts us and changes our perspective of the world around us, which helps to lower our stress levels and helps to keep our brains young and healthy.

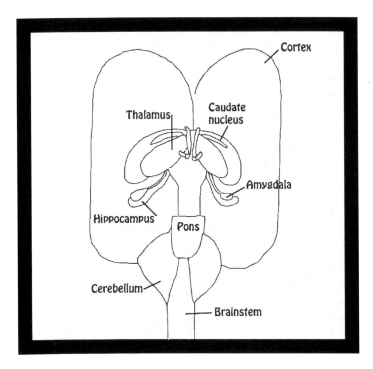

Near the hypothalamus lies the thalamus. The thalamus is the traffic cop for music and other information entering our brain. Thalamus is connected to the hypothalamus by a tract of nerves. The thalamus acts as the central switchboard for signals going to and from the spinal cord and the largest portion of the brain called the cerebrum. The thalamus filters and channels information for processing. The thalamus is connected to the cortex through a thin membrane that connects neurons to each other. Without the thalamus, we would be unable to form new, long lasting memories. Studies have shown that music enhances our long-term memory by lowering the threshold for neuron firing. In other words, because of music, the metaphoric neuron balloon holds less air before it pops and sends a message to the next neuron to imprint a new memory. Music helps the imprinting of memories by making it easier to activate sustained communication between neurons. Music does this by stimulating many sensory receptors and inducing the imprinting of memories in several different regions of the brain at the same time.

Surrounding the thalamus is a cluster of nerve cells called the basal ganglia, which processes rhythm, stress, and intonation, and help us to move to the music. They are also responsible for initiating and integrating repetitive movements and behaviors like swaying to the music. Arousing, exciting music entrains, or synchronizes, our motor circuits to fire at the same time as our emotional and reasoning brain. The firing of all of the neurons in stride with each other creates a synchronized wave pattern. Rhythmic and dynamic features like drums and cymbals can kick these circuits on. The basal ganglia activate our motor responses to music, like tapping our foot or swaying to the music. This can synchronize everyone in the room, causing harmonized swaying and mood.

The cochlea bone in our ear is directly connected to our auditory cortex and to our basal ganglia. This is the reason why dancing, singing and listening to music can feel so good. The basal ganglia connect sound input directly to our motor control and our pleasure perceptions. It is the reason why we can dance. Without this cluster of neurons, we could not keep a beat. The basal ganglia couple motor and auditory inputs to allow us to learn to speak too. We share this ability with whales, dolphins, and birds, but not primates. Have you ever seen a cockatoo dance to music? More importantly because of this link between motor and auditory input, scientists are researching the use of music to improve language skills including reading.

Ever wonder why a special song can take you back to a specific memory so realistically that you can smell the fries cooking and the color that you were wearing? The intimate connections of the hypothalamus, thalamus, cortex and hippocampus are the reason. The tract of nerve cells that connects the hypothalamus to the thalamus also connects to the hippocampus, which is located inside of the temporal and parietal lobes. The hippocampus sends memories out to the appropriate part of brain for long-term storage and retrieval. It is also our global positioning system (GPS). It helps us to locate things and orient ours geographically. Music enhances our hippocampal GPS. Researchers have observed that animals exposed to Mozart completed mazes faster, with fewer mistakes. Spatial temporal (space-time) thinking and music may activate the same hippocampal neuropathways. Scientists believe that attentively listening to music containing complex patterns encourages the firing and efficiency of hippocampal neurons and initiates the formation of new synaptic connections. This may be why musicians have more linkages between the different regions of their brains.

The hippocampus is known to have high rates of neurogenesis or births of new neurons. In monkeys, it appears that about 40% of new neurons are added after birth. Cell proliferation and neurogenesis continue in significant levels in adult monkeys. Neurogenesis continues in humans for the entire life of individuals, if the correct stimulation is provided. Music can be such a stimulus depending on whether or not we enjoy the music we are playing, dancing or listening to.

Our midbrain, which lies in the middle of our brains, is part of the reason we feel elation and joy when we sing and praise. Though it is the smallest portion of our brain, the midbrain is associated with very important functions like vision, hearing and motor control. It helps relay the musical information we hear and see, and it produces much of the dopamine that rewards and motivates us. We feel elation and joy due to the dopamine that is released when we listen to and enjoy a positive energetic tune.

FMRI scans have charted the parts of the brain that fire when we listen to joyful, peaceful, dissonant/uneasy, or sad music. Brain Imaging shows that happy music activates the same regions of the brain as when we are experiencing pleasure and reward, physiological arousal, and the motivation to move. Sad music activates the hippocampus and amygdala. The amygdala is the same region that fires neurons when we feel fear or other negative emotions and the hippocampus is our memory control center. They are the reason that both sad and happy music can activate brain regions that are connected to introspective emotions, self-control, and attentive behavior. Maybe we should play music in our children's classroom more often to inspire these areas of the brain. An article by Chris Brewer on the Johns Hopkins University website states that music enhances learning by creating a positive learning environment that improves memory, focus, rapport, relaxation and just plain fun. Music helps us to enjoy learning.

Music can calm and synchronize the rate of our breathing and heartbeat by signaling the hindbrain. The hindbrain controls the body's vital functions such as respiration and heart rate. The cerebellum, in the hindbrain, coordinates movement and is involved in activating learned repetitive movements, like driving a stick-shifted car. The cerebellum is crucial for motor coordination and timing. When you play the piano or do a well-practiced choreographed dance, you are activating the cerebellum. Habitual motion increases the amount of neurons and dendrites wired for rote or automatic movements, and thus changes the structure of our brains. Dancing and practicing music enhances coordination.

Music touches the emotional brain. It helps us to regulate our emotional state. We respond to the world around us depending on our emotional state. Music can be helpful in maintaining a positive state and emotional control. Music enhances moods, learning, and social ability. Researchers have found that music can evoke emotions like wonder, joy, and power. Music excites part of the cortex called the insula, which is involved with self-awareness or consciousness, emotions, cognitive function and motor control. It can excite the left striatum firing dopamine and feelings of reward. It is no wonder that a song can be addicting.

Music creates different emotions with distinctive patterns of firing within different regions of the brain. As an example, music that evokes wonder exhibits a stronger activation in the hippocampus for memory, but weaker activation in the caudate of the basal ganglia for movement. While, powerful music generates greater firing in the motor cortex, pushing toward physically getting up and doing something. Songs of joy, power and wonder, release dopamine to activate feelings of pleasure and reward. It is no surprise that we are instructed so many times in the Bible to sing praises! Singing a joyful song activates our dopamine reward center. It elevates our moods. Nostalgic, peaceful or transcendent music lights up the same brain regions as when we experience beauty. Music that causes us to feel nostalgia, peacefulness, tenderness, and transcendence significantly increases activity in the areas that are linked to dopamine release and reward. It also activates our memories, introspection, decision-making, and our emotional brain that is linked to mood control. When we listen to dissonant or unsettling music, no firing for dopamine and reward is seen. Finally, sad songs are associated with significant activations in our memory areas and emotional brain. Music activates our emotional, motor, and thinking brain. Different types of music activate different areas and emotions, and the correct type of music can alleviate stress, decrease negative emotions, and make us feel great.

Music can change our brain wave patterns. Highly arousing music such as those using crashing cymbals, trumpeting horns, or high-energy rhythms activate our motor circuits. It makes us want to dance! Arousing music depends on rhythmic and dynamic features to synchronize our motor processes with our auditory and emotional brain. Synchronizing or entraining causes our brainwave frequencies to fall in step with the beat. We become part of the music. Our brainwaves play along with the rhythm. The rhythm or beat synchronizes different regions of our brain together with our whole autonomic nervous system making the whole body part of the symphony. We connect with the music and become part of the masterpiece!

The different aspects of music, such as rhythm and melody, also activate different regions of the brain. Exciting music causes a desire to move or dance. When music stimulates the emotion of power, it causes a powerful increase in the firing of the motor areas; increasing the tendency to clap to the beat. Powerful music can synchronize the marching band and the armies marching to war. This is why we can use music to motivate us to laugh, to cry, to make love or war.

The type of music that causes a particular type of emotion is specific to each individual's preferences in music. It can cause memories to come up, as well as introspection, mind wandering, and improved emotion regulation. What works for you may not work for others around you, so don't expect your parent or child to want to listen to the same music as you or to have the same reaction. One thing that does seem to make a difference in preferences is music education. If you learned about music at a young age, maybe from going to musicals, operas, concerts, or symphonies, the way music affects you will be different than a person with an uneducated ear. Music education in the schools helps children to enjoy a wider variety of music and increases emotional control and enhance brain wiring.

Researchers found that the combining of the drum rhythms with a mentor to be significantly more effective in building listening skill, emotional control and focus, in 10 year olds youths than drum circles or counselors alone. The fun and social interactions that rhythms bring alleviate stress and help build relationships. Group drumming can decrease the stress caused by social pressures. Youths that join drum circles and have someone to talk to about their problems become less withdrawn, depressed, and anxious. The drum circles improve post-traumatic stress problems and attention deficit/hyperactivity problems. The youths were less defiant and the speed of understanding and learning increased. Studies on group drumming also demonstrated decreased stress hormones and increased immunity. We should use crashing cymbals and tambourines in our schools and other social gatherings just as King David instructed.

Have you ever sung a lullaby to a child to comfort them or lull them to sleep? The rhythm of a mother's heartbeat regularly beats between 60 and 100 beats per minute, and an infant's heart beats at about 140 to 150 beats per minute. Interestingly, these are some of the same rhythmic frequencies beaten by some tribal drums around the world to bring calmness, healing, and social connectedness. Emotional responses to music are seen across all cultures and ages indicating that we are born with the ability to perceive emotions in music. Even newborns have an inborn ability to perceive music and move rhythmically to music. In a study of underweight newborns, researchers played tape-recorded vocal music, including lullabies and children's music, during the infant's stay in ICU. The music significantly increased the daily average weight and the amount of food taken, and reduced the initial weight loss, stress behaviors and the length of the hospital stays.

Researchers believe that the infant's improvement was due to the reduction of stress that music brings. This may seem like a 'no brainer' when we look at how long mothers have been singing lullabies to calm their babies. A mother's voice can protect an infant's brain from the changes that stress causes while other voices can't. A recording of a mother's voice can suppress epigenetically linked changes to dopamine and serotonin receptors even while separated. Besides the emotionally calming effects of music, musically trained children exhibit an increase in the size of gray and/or white matter and have greater verbal abilities than other children their own age with no musical training. Singing to your children and providing a varied musical experience is essential to your child's development.

Music works for patients of all ages. A study published in the Journal of American Medical Association reported significant decreases in anxiety and sedatives in ventilated patients listening to self-chosen music, using headphones, 80 minutes a day. Pleasurable music soothes fear and pain.

Music keeps our brains young; so use it to turn sadness into joy and sorrow to celebration and comfort. High levels of stress, anxiety, or emotional pain are linked to addictions like overeating, smoking or drinking alcohol. Singing, dancing, playing a musical instrument, or just listening to music and tapping your foot, increases serotonin, dopamine and neurotransmitters levels that effectively lower stress, anxiety and depression. Studies show that you must consistently practice your musical abilities to sustain the rise in the hormone levels. So continually singing praises is essential, with an emphasis on continually.

Music reduces the anxiety, depression and aggressiveness in Alzheimer's patients and has helped with recall. In many cases, a patient may remember songs when everything else is forgotten. The reduction of anxiety and depression can be observed in as little as 4 weeks in many Alzheimer's patients, but sometimes it may be immediate.

Today scientists are using brain-imaging scans to see how the brain and body is affected by song. They have combined imaging with the psychophysiological measurements of skin temperature and resistance, respiration, muscle movement, and heart rate. Combined tests measure the functions of the body while linking them with the behaviors and emotions of the mind. The results of these tests have led scientists to believe that the emotions that are elicited by music affect the whole body.

An emotionally charged song is received through our ears, is assessed by our brains, and fires messengers through our whole autonomic system. These messages affect our pain/pleasure system and motivate us to move. Our muscles respond through dancing, clapping, swaying, or facial expressions such as smiling or frowning depending on how our emotions are perceived. Listening to music reduces heart rate, respiratory rate, and blood pressure. In Psalm 108:1, David tells us, "My heart is steadfast, O God; I will sing and make music with all my soul". Music steadies the heart rate and protects the body. Consistent listening or singing can also reduce pain levels by releasing endorphins, our bodies' homemade opium.

The emotional affects of music and rhythms may be universal. Music may use mirror neurons to stimulate emotions. Neuroimaging shows that certain mirror neurons activities are enhanced during the imitation of emotional facial expressions and during musically evoked emotional states. These same regions may also activate for bodily states such as pain and hunger. Music can activate these regions in children as young as 3 years of age. People from different cultures react to the music as if they are familiar and understood the type of music that they are listening to. The basis for such a powerful universal reaction, especially to sad and happy emotions in music, is probably rooted in the acoustic features of music. Happy music is characterized by fast tempo and major mode, whereas sad music is typically played in slow tempo and minor mode. Music activates the same regions in our brains that fire while processing emotions and premeditating a reward. People everywhere can create a mood and change their emotional state simply listening to the right style of music.

How do tempo and other features of music affect our brains? Musical rhythms, including tempo and dynamic acoustical features like a drumbeat, volume variations or the pulse of a swing, change our spontaneous brain activity. Spontaneous activity is brain activity that takes place when we are in a state of rest. This continuous under-current of brain activity tells us about the current mental state of the person. Brainwave patterns tell us how alert a person is, or whether a person is asleep or dreaming. Rhythmic or repetitive neural activities in the central nervous system called neural oscillations are responsible for measurable brainwaves. The activity of a group or network of neurons and the synchronized firing of different regions of the brain can be measured by electroencephalography (EEG) and without touching the skin by magnetoencephalography (MEG). An example of the synchronized firing of different regions of our brain is the alpha waves, which repeats at 8-12 Hz. Alpha activity can be detected in the occipital lobe during relaxation. This rhythmic brain activity has been linked to information transfer, motor control, memory and perception. Other frequency bands besides alpha are: delta at 1-4 Hz, theta at 4-8 Hz, beta at 13-30 Hz, and gamma at 30-70 Hz. The lower frequencies, like alpha, delta and theta, are linked to deep sleep and the faster frequencies, like beta, are linked to cognitive processes.

Spontaneous neural oscillations or waves generate rhythmic activity such as heartbeat. Waves of nerves firing at the same time help us perceive the shape, color and gestalt of objects. These oscillations have been linked to many disorders such as tremors in Parkinson's disease or seizures in epilepsy, which is an excess of synchronization. Musical beats stimulate rhythms in our brainwave patterns. Musical rhythms cause a synchronization, or unified firing of our neural groups and brain regions. Rhythms even unify the firing of different areas of our brain to each other. This synchronistic firing of the auditory and motor regions of the brain may be responsible for the yearning to tap our foot or dance when we hear music.

The rhythms of music adjust our moods and thoughts by changing our brainwave patterns. Using magnetoencephalography to measure wave activity during passive listening, one study found that an accented rhythmic beat consistently caused a decrease in wave activity, which was immediately followed by an increase. This consistent up and down pattern in our brainwaves causes our brains to synchronize with the musical rhythms. Brainwaves are our brains' way of communicating cues for motor actions such as dancing. Studies combining EEGs and other physiological tests such as skin permeability, and heart and respiratory rate, show that different brainwaves are related to different levels of relaxation, agitation, and sleep. EEGs also prove that music changes our brainwaves, explaining why music has such profound affects on our emotions. Music, through the synchronization of our brainwaves, truly makes 'our ear bone connected to our foot bone'.

The affects of music are universal across all cultures. Whether music is: sung as a lullaby, danced to in a social setting, or listened to in order to relax, all cultures incorporate it into life. Since music can synchronize the brainwaves, heartbeat and respiration of one person, just visualize what music can do to a group of people that are fully engaged, like those praising together. Music can change the use of our genes, rewire our nervous system and unify the brainwaves of a group. Unification of brain wave patterns in a group helps with communication, community cohesion, and social interactions. This explains the swaying room, the feeling of a praise choir, and the behavior of a moshe pit.

Brainwaves not only affect but are also affected by neurotransmitters. Certain neurotransmitters regulate the frequency and amplitude of the brainwaves. Neurotransmitters like serotonin, acetylcholine, norepinephrine and GABA affect our moods and emotions. Music has been shown to increase the release of certain mood enhancing neurotransmitters. One of the messengers released while music listening at its emotional peak was dopamine. Dopamine is the messenger that tells our brain to anticipate and be motivated for rewards. It creates cravings. Intense pleasure or that goose bumpy feeling that certain music brings us can lead to dopamine release both when anticipating the music and from the musical climax itself. Our bodies' perceive positive, emotionally charged music as a reward much the same way as being offered a prize. Music releases dopamine just as if we received an offer to win money or receive a favorite food. Music activates the same parts of our brains as chocolate, opium and sexual orgasm. We can use music when we are depressed, anxious or bored instead of picking up that favorite food. We can sing praises of love, gratitude and strength instead of picking up our favorite addiction.

Dopamine is not the only messenger that is released while listening to music. If the music is soothing, it can increase the listener's level of oxytocin. According to Dr. Daniel Levitin, professor of psychology and neuroscience at McGill University, singing increases oxytocin. Oxytocin is the hormone that is linked with sexual climax, love and relationship bonding. Serotonin and certain neurotransmitters increase after 4 weeks of singing and movement and decrease when you stop. Oxytocin is known as the love messenger and is important in the formation of social attachments and relationships. Soothing lullabies can cause the release of oxytocin in both the mother and the child, helping to strengthen the bond between them. So parents sing to your children. The family that sings together stays together!

Music can influence our emotional states, which in turn influence our perception of the world. The oxytocin that is released by musical elation aids in social bonding. Not only does oxytocin release help to build bonds between dancers and singers in a social atmosphere but the synchronization of brainwaves can affect the whole group by entraining the brainwaves of each individual to the music. If each person is entrained to the same music, the group is synchronized together through the music. Now, if you add the awe inspiring of a spectacular praise song, you can add oxytocin to the mix and end up with a very cohesive and loving group of people. This is what the Divine envisioned for us. Dancing, playing, and singing of praises build relationships and bonds. Some scientists believe that musical behavior is adaptive because it promotes group cohesion causing synchronized actions, emotions, and a positive group identity. Several hundred species of birds perform precisely synchronized duets in order to reproduce, strengthen partnership bonds, or defend territories. Certain species of insects, like crickets and frogs, practice synchronized chorusing. The repeated and predictable rhythms and melodies in music and dance help unify focus, emotions and expectations. Music helps us to love one another.

Singing lowers cortisol levels, raises immunity and enhances mood. When people have fun or play at making music, it stimulates the immune system in both younger and older people. It raises t-cells, lymphocytes, and controls the production of interferon and interleukin to help to control tumors and inflammation, inhibit viruses, and speed immune responses during infection or trauma. The positive emotional boost and the decrease of stress hormones that music evokes, enhances our immunity. It makes you wonder why all medical facilities aren't playing Mozart or something!

Music can change our heart rate and heart rate variability. It can steady our heart and make it jump. Certain kinds of music help to regulate cardiac functions by causing stress-reducing affects. So music, through playing, dancing, singing, clapping, or other forms of participation, can be used to achieve positive physiological states by influencing our emotions. The main point is that you must be having fun! If you hate classical music or punk rock, they won't help you. The type of music required to achieve positive results, varies according to the listener's preferences and musical education.

When one is completely wrapped up in listening to music, it is more effective in reducing stress than progressive muscle relaxation and focused imagery. Playing pre and postoperative music is beneficial to patients undergoing open-heart surgery. In fact, if music is used before the operation, it significantly decreases the level of anxiety of the patients. Music can be an effective alternative to medications normally given to relax a patient before surgery and music has the added benefit of causing none of the adverse effects of some medications. After the surgery, music continues to decrease cortisol levels and helps to lower heart and respiratory rates, especially when using vocal or orchestral music. Heavy metal or techno music may cause dangerous arrhythmias and stress in certain patients. The right kinds of music stabilize blood pressure and entrain heart rate. Music has been shown to enhance the quality of sleep in newborns. In Psalms 16, verse 9, David said, "Therefore my heart is glad and my tongue rejoices; my body also will rest secure". King David noted that singing helps our hearts and helps us sleep peacefully, long before science could prove it.

Music, whether we are singing, dancing, listening or playing it, affects our emotional, physical, and mental well-being. When we are swept away by it, music can cause awe or elation. It can cause goose bumps or tears. It changes the way our genes make our proteins, the way our brains are wired, and the rate in which our neurons fire. **Music can unify us together as one in love.** Music powerfully guides our emotional states, bringing joy when there is sorrow, makes our hearts strong, and our sleep peaceful. Like the grass waving together in the breeze, a flock of birds moving in unity or the rhythmic waves of the ocean, joyful music gathers our hearts and minds together as one creating harmony. So sing a joyful noise!

Love One Another

Social interactions keep our brains healthy and youthful. The Bible told us to gather together, hold each other up, and to love one another. These are the very things that help to protect our genes from unwanted epigenetic changes that can product problems with our physical, mental and emotional health. Scientists have found that a rich social environment is beneficial to turning on the genes that enable us to produce brain-derived neurotrophic factor (BDNF), one of the peptides that aid in neurogenesis. Neurogenesis is the proliferation, differentiation, migration and survival of new neurons in our brains. BDNF is a growth factor that is essential for proper brain development. A 2008 study showed that deleting a BDNF receptor alters the way newborn neurons integrate into hippocampal circuitry impairing memory function. Decreased BDNF receptors reduce the growth of dendrite and spines and decrease neural connections, and increases anxiety-like behaviors. This study demonstrates how important adult neurogenesis is to regulating our moods. Social relations with people that we care about and care about us help to grow new neurons enhancing memory and mood.

Researchers have discovered that early social environments modify the epigenetics of our children. We are told in 1 John 4 verse 12 to love each other because God lives in us, and his love is expressed through us. We are temples of God's love. Expressing and receiving love is critical to our physical, mental and emotional health. How much we are cherished as children alters the amounts of certain proteins in our bodies. In fact, how much we are nurtured by our early caretakers influences our hypothalamic-pituitary-adrenal (HPA) function by epigenetically lowering the amount of glucocorticoid receptors that are made. This HPA function is related to a hyperactive fight or flight response. Fewer receptors equal more fear. The fear inhibition freeways are knocked out. But, we can stop our fear and anxiety. Love and nurturing makes us less reactive by increasing the receptors. Love truly casts out fear.

This is how the epigenetic mechanism works. The number of receptors is decreased because its gene is not being copied. This happens because epigenetic stop signs, called methyl groups, are attached over the starting point or promoter for that receptor's gene. A methyl group is a carbon with three oxygen groups attached to it. Too many methyl groups crowd the gene and make it difficult to start the DNA copying machinery. These methyl groups tighten the coiled DNA and silence the gene. This happens because all the factors needed to start copying can't get to the crowded initiation code. This lowers the amount of glucocorticoid receptors found in our brains. Lack of nurturing reduces hippocampal glucocorticoid receptors making us highly reactive to environmental stresses. Without love, fear is programmed into our brains. We need love!

In humans, lowered levels these receptors are linked to higher levels of suicide, major depression and anxiety. Reduced receptors are found in suicide victims with a history child abuse. Stresses in early life coincides with abnormal expression of the serotonin transporter gene as well as decreased expression of the brain-derived neurotrophic factor's promoter. Unfortunately, the tests that show the lower levels of receptors in humans were done postmortem, after the suicides. Tests on human brains are very difficult to do when the subject is alive so most of our information comes from the tests scientist run on animals leaving room for argument about the efficacy of certain medications. The bottom line is that low levels of serotonin and BDNF are linked to depression, anxiety and suicide. The attention and care one receives as an infant changes our epigenetic mechanisms. Children need to be loved. Love changes how our DNA is made into RNA and then to peptides and proteins. Love can prevent depression.

One of the most amazing things that scientists have found is that the epigenetic changes in the way our genes are copied can be changed back. By using different natural things such as plants, we can pull off or replace the methyl groups or acetyl groups, and turn on or off the affected genes. We now know that certain enzymes are able to remove or add methyl groups, acetyl groups, or small microRNA from our DNA, histones or RNA. RNA is ribonucleic acid, which is the newly copied piece of the gene used to construct amino acids. When these epigenetic groups are removed or added, genes can be turned on or off. These changes happen especially in very young infants but researchers have also revealed that silenced gene promoters can be switched back on even in adults. We can control how our genes are used!

The plant foods we eat can help us to alter how our genes are copied. One enzyme, used to switch genes back on, is named histone deacetylase inhibitor (HDACi). HDACi stops the removal of acetyl groups, which increases the acetyl groups on the histones. This activates the chromatin, or coiled DNA packages, leading to the loss of a methyl group on the DNA framework, reversing of the gene deactivation. HDACi turns the silenced gene back on by loosening the coiling of the DNA, which alleviates the crowding and allows the copying to begin again.

Why is turning silenced genes back on so important? Silenced genes can lead to cancer, aging, rheumatoid pain, depression and even suicide. Researchers found that HDCAi enzymes given for one week to hyper-vigilant or highly fearful adult rats that were reared by non-nurturing caretakers, completely changed the corticosterone responses. The enzymes were so successful; their responses were indistinguishable from adult rats that were raised by nurturing mothers. Their fear responses and stress levels were brought back to a normal state, alleviating anxiety and depressive states. Histone deacetylase inhibitors (HDACi) have also been reported to inhibit tumor formation and to induce apoptosis or cell death in cancer cells.

Remarkably, these enzymes are contained in many foods and herbs. HDACi is found in many foods and herbs that are easily accessible, such as broccoli and its sprouts, wheat grass sprouts, hops, and valerian root just to name a few. We can even stop depression and anxiety with the food we eat and the herbs we take without the expense and side effects of pharmaceutical medications.

Loving others and ourselves can provide health and happiness. Believe it or not our enzymes help us to love. Scientists tell us that pheromones help us fall passionately in love. Pheromones are enzymes that we give off and are picked up by others. Amit Gowami, a physicist from the University of Oregon, hypothesizes that one of the things that pheromones do when we fall in love, is to help our cells to recognize the other person as ourselves. Our cells see, or rather smell, the one that we are in love with as being part of the same entity as us. Just like single-celled animals recognize their divided daughter cells as themselves and protect them with their own lives; we recognize our loved ones as self. Loving others as ourselves is really taking caring of our body temple. Research has revealed that when a person falls in love, the brain releases euphoria-inducing chemicals including oxytocin, dopamine, vasopression and adrenaline. It raises levels of nerve growth factor, which enhances body image and other cognitive brain functions.

Mother love or passionate love each stimulates different parts of the brain. The science of epigenetics has illuminated the importance of mother love, and other kinds of love, to our epigenetic health, both when we are newborns and later in life. Wouldn't it be wonderful if we could recognize everyone in the world as self and truly love each one? After all, aren't we made of the same Divine Energy? With this one change in belief, we would automatically improve our body image, how we perceive things, and enhance our higher brain functions and health. All these improvements because we finally understand the science behind what the Bible said as a literal truth. Ephesians 4 verse 4, told us, "There is one body, and one Spirit, even as ye are called in one hope of your calling." Maybe this is literally telling us that there is one universal body and one universal energy Spirit making it all work. The quality of our relationships and the amount of love we give and receive, not only guards our genetic code but it can enhance our chances of living an emotionally and physically healthy life.

Loving Others as Ourselves

Mirror neurons are special cells in our brains that we use to learn to walk and act by mimicking others. We use them to learn empathy for others too. Our mirror neurons remind us that we are one. When we see a homeless person somewhere inside we feel fear. Because, deep down we are aware that if one person is homeless, then there is always a chance that we or someone we love could become homeless. Mirror neurons remind when we see suffering that we too can suffer. If anyone is hungry, cold or in pain, our mirror neuron transmit to our brains and bodies the emotions of others. If anyone suffers on earth we are all in danger of suffering. Like the ability to wipe out small pox from the earth so no one will ever need to fear contracting it again, we have the ability to wipe out hunger and homelessness so no one will ever feel it or fear it again. Positive emotions like love, gratitude and helping others, positively affects our health. When we take care of others we are really taking care of ourselves. Doing something nice is as easy as saying something kind. King Solomon in Proverbs 15, verse 13, knew this. He told us, "Gracious words are a honey comb, sweet to the soul and healing to the bones". It heals others and us too.

Epigenetics studies have revealed that not only do we need to be loved from the moment we are born, but doing good deeds for others also gives us huge rewards. These rewards include: a release of natural opiates, called endorphins, dopamine, which is the neurotransmitter that is related to reward and pleasure, and oxytocin, which gives our hearts a lift. In Isaiah 58, verse 10, it is written, "if you spend yourselves in behalf of the hungry and satisfy the needs of the oppressed, then your light will rise in the darkness, and your night will become like the noonday". Doing a good deed gives others and us energy. Have you ever watched a good deed? Doesn't it make everyone feel great? The Divine is giving us a recipe for how to fill ourselves up with energy and Divine energy is what gives us life.

People who are charitable toward others often have high levels of the hormone, oxytocin. Increased levels of oxytocin may trigger the release of dopamine and endorphins from the heart and the brain, which is why we feel euphoric when we feel love. Dr. J. Andrew Armour, a leading neurocardiologist on Institute of HearthMath's Scientific Advisory Board, found that the heart contains cells that synthesize and release hormones such as epinephrine (adrenaline), dopamine, and others. More recently, it was discovered that the heart also secretes oxytocin, commonly referred to as the "love" or "bonding" hormone. Remarkably, concentrations of oxytocin produced in the heart are as high as those found in the brain. Just as we were told in Proverbs 17 verse 22, "A cheerful heart is good medicine". A good deed is good for your heart literally!

Dr. James Danielli found that doing, watching or receiving good deeds, are ways to release mood-controlling substances, which are like opium, into the brain and elsewhere in the body. This internal reward system can be used anytime you are feeling down. Take some books to a retirement home, serve food at a food bank or just help your neighbor. All of these will reward you with a great feeling and a healthier heart, and the best part is that if someone else is watching, they will feel good too!

Studies have shown that disorders with oxytocin and vasopressin receptors contribute to a lack of social skills in people with autism. Increased social interactions can boost the expression (or constructing) of these receptors, so the more social we become, the more receptors we make. We need to gather together. It is written in Hebrews 10 verses 24 and 25, "And let us consider how to stir up one another to good works, not neglecting to meet together". Getting together feels good and rewires our brains and bodies to run better. We learn empathy, and even to walk, by watching others. The more we get together the better we get at it, and like the old preschool song says, " the more we get together, the happier we'll be".

In Colossians 3, verses 14 and 15, we are told to "put on love, which is the perfect bond of unity". Whether brought on by music, meditation or shared media, emotions unify us using neurotransmitters and brainwaves. Our minds can work as one to bring peace or war, and fear or love, depending on what we focus on. Its no accident that we are told in Philippians 4, verse 8 to dwell on whatever is true, right, pure, lovely, admirable, excellent and praiseworthy. Our bodies are unified through oxytocin, mirror neurons and chemical scents. Loving one another is one of the healthiest things we can do for our physical and emotional health. If we actually accepted what our bodies are telling us, we could truly "love our neighbors as ourselves".

Gratitude

Gratitude, when practiced on a daily basis, teaches us to trust. Counting your blessings helps us to be aware of the positive things in our lives. We begin to see the glass half full. Over time by taking note of the good that happens, we can begin to build a trust that things will work out for the best and our core beliefs can change. We can begin to believe that all things do work together!

Hebrews 12, verse 28 reminds us to "let us be grateful for receiving a kingdom that cannot be shaken". We are part of the kingdom of energy so great that it makes up the universe. We receive this universal energy every second of our lives. The awareness of the power that runs through our temples is amplified when we acknowledge it daily. The rest of verse 28 told us to offer praise, reverence and awe. These are all states of mind that aid us in emotional and physical health.

Our beliefs control how our bodies react to external and internal stimuli. If we are always waiting and worrying about the future, and stewing about the past, our bodies will react with fear. Whether we like it or not, negative thoughts and beliefs throw us into fight or flight. These stress hormones cause havoc in our bodies. The fear and stress that follows controls how our receptor cells react to the stimuli. These reactions are sent as messages to tell the rest of our cells what is going on around us. How we perceive the things our senses receive, instructs our proteins and RNA on how to copy our genes. Our beliefs control the building blocks of our bodies. We were designed to remember the positive things, in awe each day. David had it right! In Psalm 103, verses 1-5, he wrote, "Bless the Lord, O my soul, and all that is within me, bless his holy name! Forget not all his benefits, who forgives, who heals all your diseases, who saves your life from the pit, who satisfies so that your youth is renewed".

Have you ever thought about what you mean when you say, "No, thank you"? You are rejecting something. No matter how nicely you say it, you are putting your hand up and saying "stop, I don't want this". Inversely, when you say "thank you," you are accepting something. No matter how grimly you mumble it, it means you accept what is going on or being offered.

The Bible directs us "In everything give thanks, for this is the will of God." Does this mean for us to accept things? Some translations of 1 Thessalonians 5, verse 18, shared precisely that, "give thanks in all circumstances, for this is the will of God". Does this mean we shouldn't try to better our circumstances or ourselves? No, it just tells us that our present moment is the will of God and that accepting where we are today is also God's will.

I remember the first time I really understood this concept. I was really upset over a relationship that was ending and told a friend at church, "I just wish everything was OK". She looked at me and responded, "It already is OK, because what is, just is". That statement changed everything! You can't argue. What already exists at the present moment just exists. Acceptance of the moment, or rather positive acceptance of where we are, helps us to feel comfortable in our own skin. If you understand where you are starting from, getting from there to where you want to be becomes possible. Have you ever been lost when you are going somewhere? It is impossible to go where you want if you don't know where you are! Until you get your bearing, you can't know which direction you need to go to arrive to your desired destination. Arguing with God's will is like arguing with the fire department's air tanker pilot when you are caught in a firestorm, the pilot can see how to get out but you can't. Arguing will most likely lead to a lot of pain and suffering. Paul in Acts 24, verse 3 wrote, " In every way and everywhere we accept this with all gratitude". Acceptance of the present moment, right where you are at, helps you to understand your starting point so you can arrive at your desired destination.

Gratitude is accepting what has been given to you, hopefully with a positive attitude. Studies supported by the National Institutes of Health found that teenagers that counted their blessings or practiced being thankful fell into restful sleep. Gratitude also puts you in a more positive mindset. It is a proven way to self-heal or self-regulate mood when you are depressed. A Swiss study found that practicing gratitude exhibited more benefits the older one gets. Practicing gratitude accurately predicts health and well-being as one ages. A general state of appreciation or thankfulness increases a sense of well-being, better relationships, and lowers stress levels.

Expressing gratitude makes others feel good about themselves, and increases their feelings of social worth. The old adage 'return a complement with a complement' is true. It makes people feel valued. When we help someone, it helps us feel empathy and feel good about ourselves. Counting our blessings increases a positive outlook no matter your situation. Einstein said, "You can't solve a problem on the level on which it was created." Gratitude changes the level of thinking. It changes core beliefs.

Acceptance of what is happening isn't saying that is what we want to be happening but only acknowledges that it already is happening. If something is already occurring you can't say that it isn't. Acceptance places us in the present moment without arguing in our heads. Acceptance clears our mind of negative thoughts and puts us in a more positive mood. In 1 Thessalonians 5, verses 16-18, we are instructed to "Be joyful always; pray continually; give thanks in all circumstances". Prayer, joy, and gratitude will guard our hearts and brains from disease by decreasing stress. Practicing gratitude or counting blessings causes us to become more aware of the positive things in our lives. It conditions us to look for the good things that happen, sort of like looking for the red VW. You start to see it everywhere. Start seeking and you will find things to be grateful about and pretty soon you will find your mood elevated too. The fascinating thing is that if you believe what Paul wrote in Romans 8, verse 28, "that all things work together for the good of them that love God," your belief aids in your gratitude. Equally, your practice of gratitude will help to build your trust and beliefs.

Although, some of us practice acceptance each day, others of us practice the opposite, which is called denial. Denial puts us in a place of blindness, like the proverbial ostrich with its head in the sand. Gratitude means accepting things with positive feeling toward those who have given to us. In every circumstance, we are to accept where we are in that moment. Acknowledge that where we are, is our starting place, whether it is a good circumstance or an unfavorable one. Only when we can accept our present happening can we move on emotionally. Many of us stay stuck for a very long time because we can't accept our circumstances. We can become lost in the emotions of denial or rejection. "It merely is what it is and that's what it is". It seems ridiculous that we fight against the already present moment, when gratitude and acceptance are the true start of change. Happily, we are instructed to be thankful in all circumstances.

Worry

Ecclesiastes 11, verse 10 began, "So refuse to worry, and keep your body healthy." This is pretty straightforward, not much explanation is needed. We know that chronically elevated stress hormones lead to chronic illnesses. So why do so many of us still worry? Why does worry seem to be so hard to control when we know that stress does so much harm to our bodies?

What is worry? Worry is a repetitive circular thinking pattern, where we are trying to premeditate and solve problems, even before they happen. Worry is voluntary! Worry and anxiety are different. Unlike anxiety, which is a state initiated by fear that causes a cascade of chemical reactions and sustained high levels of stress hormones, worry is a learned thought process that can be unlearned. This thought process is often turned on by what we premeditate or assume may happen. In other words, what we image might happen. These imagined issues or dangers affect us physically. Imagined or perceived danger is one of the largest causes of increased stress responses in our bodies.

Why do we worry when Matthew 6 verse 27 asked us: "Who of you by worrying can add a single hour to his life?" Worry or premeditation of dangers, whether imagined or otherwise, is how we adapt and survive. We have all heard the story of the person that walks down the street and falls into a hole and takes all day to get out. The next day, the same person falls in the same hole but is able to get out of the hole much faster. The following day, the person walks down a different street to avoid the hole. This is a story of adaptation and the quicker we adapt to situations; the better able we are to survive socially, financially, emotionally and physically. It is how we learn to get along.

In the past, if a bear appeared in the same thicket that we walked in the day before, if we were smart, we premeditated that she would be there again and stayed out of that thicket. Worry worked for us, we premeditated, we adapted, and we survived another day. This ability to adapt is still important to us today, though most of the time it is not life threatening as it may have been in the past. Modern humans use adaptation to learn to get along with others in social situations. We learn what acceptable behavior is, and what gets us punished or shunned by others. As adults, we use our adaptive skills in new situations constantly, and those of us that are best at it are often leaders, negotiators, and skilled business people.

The problem begins when we become caught in a repetitive cycle of trying to sidestep imagined, premeditated future situations. In Matthew 6 verse 34 reminded us "not to worry about tomorrow, for tomorrow will worry about itself. Each day has enough trouble of its own". Young children learn to adapt without rethinking the changes over and over. It is the repetitive thought and not the adaptations or changes in behavior patterns that affect our health.

Worry is a learned voluntary thought process that becomes habitual. It is a function of our cortex or thinking brain, and thankfully, the cortex is where we can re-teach our brain. Repetitive negative thoughts can switch on the amygdala, our brains' fear center. This can lead to negative emotions rushing chemicals to the hypothalamus and to the adrenals to elevate cortisol levels. Chronic worry can even change our epigenetic code and alter how fight or flight genes are expressed. These alterations have been found in people with posttraumatic stress disorder, anxiety, and depression.

Sometimes this worry switch can even get stuck in the on position, leading to problems like obsessive and compulsive worrying. Getting stuck in the on position makes us unable to change what we are thinking. This leads to circular thoughts and can turn on our cingulate gyrus. The cingulate gyrus, a ridge in the middle of our cerebral cortex, causes that wrenching feeling in our Guts that accompanies dread. It can even affect our thalamus, which controls how we perceive the things that are happening around us.

Our cortex is one part of our brains that is plastic or malleable. We have some control over it through our beliefs and thought patterns. Most of us contemplate things that haven't happened and often will never happen. Somehow, some of us have even learned that negative thoughts are beneficial. I have heard people say that if they worry about something it never comes true, as if their worrying magically stopped bad things from happening. Worrying gives us a false sense of doing something when we are not.

Certainly anticipating real dangers are important to our survival and are correlated to intelligence levels. But, chronic worry leads to all of the same problems that chronic stress is associated with. Chronic worrying decreases brain density and neural connections. It also decreases immunity and lifespan, and leads to premature aging, changes in gene expression, and an increase in a multitude of diseases. Rationally going over options and decision-making is an adaptive tool that keeps our brains healthy. It is an adaptive tool use for the survival of our species. But, chronic or circular worry does the opposite. Who of us by worrying can add a single hour to his life? Science now tells us that we actually shorten our lives by chronically worrying.

Knowing that worrying is destructive to our health, why do we still worry? Worry is a learned process. If your parents or caretakers were worriers, chances are you are a worrier too. The good thing is, if we can learn it, we can unlearn it. Research from UCLA has displayed through PET scans that people who are stuck in obsessive stress can become unstuck in as little as 10 weeks using behavioral therapy. These people were chronic worriers. These scans prove that chronic worry can be stopped. Combining measurements of heart and respiratory rate with brainwave measurements, show that self-regulation of negative thought patterns can have positive effects on our nervous systems and overall health. We can stop our own negative thinking.

The main technique used to stop worry is education. This includes the reviewing of positive and negative beliefs about worry. It helps to become aware of what initiates worry by identifying its triggers. By learning to let go of worry, allotting specific times of the day to worry, substituting problem-solving techniques in place of worry, and use of meditation, prayer, or relaxation exercises, chronic worriers were able to make marked changes in their brains. Proverbs 3, verse 5 instructed us to "Trust in the Lord with all your heart and lean not on your own understanding." Learning to stop trying to figure every little detail out is very difficult. If you're like me, if one little detail doesn't fit, I am trying to figure out why. Setting up a time limit on ruminating or worrying about this is important but even more important is the ability to let go and trust that all things work together, even when I can't understand how it will work out. Times up, time to let go!

These are not the only ways to help un-stick chronic worriers. The arts are an affective way to repair our moods. Studies have shown that creative outlets can be more affective in causing positive moods than venting with words. In Psalm 57, verse 7, David said, "my heart is steadfast, I will sing and make music". Science today shows that singing and making music makes the heart feel strong. Praising works through the dynamics of the music and the emotions connected with it such as awe or peace.

Our emotions are controlled by our beliefs. Our positive and negative beliefs about: the Divine, the world, others, and ourselves make a difference in how much we worry. Beliefs also affect other dysfunctions such as anxiety, depression, and even low self-esteem. What we believe about a higher power is truly important! "Trust in the Lord God with all of your heart and lean not on your understanding". Do you have faith even if your logical mind doesn't really understand who God is? 2 Corinthians 9, verse 8 told us that, "God will generously provide all you need. Then you will always have everything you need and plenty left over to share with others." Believing that God is generous and there is always enough for everyone allows us to stop worrying.

Self-esteem and self-image control our emotions. What do you believe about yourself? 1 Corinthians 3 verses 16 and 17 asked, "Don't you realize that you are the temple of God, and that the Spirit of God lives in you?" We are temples of the Holy Spirit! We are vessels that hold infinite energy. Today, studies in quantum physics give us the basis for realizing that an infinite source of energy that provides everything. Understanding science builds our trust. We no longer simply need faith to believe.

How do we view ourselves? Can we connect to what it feels like to be temples of that Divine Energy? In 1 Corinthians 3, verse 16, Paul asked, "Don't you know that you yourselves are God's temple and that God's Spirit lives in you?" The importance of understanding this identity about ourselves cannot be overstated! Connecting to that identity is how we can gain the power of the Holy Spirit or infinite energy. It is inside each one of us. Ephesians 3:20, "Now unto him that is able to do exceeding abundantly above all that we ask or think, according to the power that worketh in us". He worked power in us! If you look up worked in the dictionary, it is defined as 'made with craft and skill'. So you and I are made with craft and skill to contain power. That is how special each one of us is to the Divine.

How do we build trust in a single unified energy field? Psalm 46, verse 10 told us "Be still and know that I am God". The structure of the brain is altered through quieting our minds. This can be done through meditation, chanting, and deep prayer. Another way to connect to infinite energy is to become aware of rhythms of nature. Meditative walking or running is a great way to come to a quiet state. Habakkuk 2, verse 14, described a world filled with the awareness of the Divine. "For as the waters fill the sea, the earth will be filled with an awareness of the glory of the LORD". Spending time in nature can also change the brainwaves that our brains use most often.

Becoming quiet in a natural environment can change your brainwave patterns. Brainwaves can be measured by electroencephalograms (EEGs). They tell us the state of relaxation or stimulation the mind is in. Different personality traits are linked to different wave patterns. We have all heard about Type A personalities being generalized as aggressive, competitive go-getters. Type A personalities use the Beta waves (12Hz or higher) most often. Chronic Beta waves can lead to worry, anxiety and depression. They can also lead to a loss of sleep, focus, memory, and the ability to really be present to listen and participate in one's own life.

Theta waves are slower, about 4 to 8hertz. They are the best wave patterns to use when we are re-learning beliefs. Theta oscillations are one of the waves measured when we meditate. Scientists believe that theta waves modulate the firing of hippocampal neurons. The hippocampus is involved in memory formation. It is believed hippocampus indexes our memories and sends them out for long-term storage. In fact, our memories epigenetically change the DNA in our brain cells by hanging new acetyl groups. The hippocampus is part of our emotional brain and is particularly important in connecting emotions and senses, such as smell and sound, to new memories. This was especially imperative to hunter-gatherers. Remembering where you saw a bear is very important to surviving in nature and the writing of new responses for social adaptation are equally important. Being still, whether by prayer, meditation or simply walking quietly through nature brings our brains into theta waves to stop worry, anxiety and depression.

Robert Monroe of the Monroe Institute in Virginia found that addictive behaviors, such as chronic worrying, could be stopped permanently using enriched environments. 17 out of 20 participants were freed from addictions using guided sessions combining the sounds of the ocean, birds, running water, or music with a verbal narrative, and followed by physical exercise. This technique uses both alpha and theta wave training to change the brainwaves. It sure sounds a lot like playing outside in nature and using your imagination, doesn't it? This is an example of using enriched environments to change the brain. Why not utilize nature, a park, a garden or an ocean or forest to rewrite your own story and become aware of the Divine Spirit in everything? Sit under a tree and meditate. Remember the fact that everything is interactions and vibrations of one infinite energy field. Walk being mindful of the trees, birds, breezes and the emptiness between them.

How we view the world around us is also important to whether we worry or not. Is the world around you friendly or inhospitable? Is it a neutral world, are you lucky, or is the world conspiring against you? This may sound funny but our beliefs can be heard in our language. We may call it 'Murphy

Law' and say that 'anything that can go wrong will go wrong'. Or, are you one of those people that believe that you were 'born under a lucky star' and that the world is always sending you luck? Matthew 6 verses 30-31 asked, "And if God cares so wonderfully for wildflowers that are here today and thrown into the fire tomorrow, he will certainly care for you. Why do you have so little faith? So don't worry about these things, saying, what will we eat? What will we drink? What will we wear?" Stop worrying and start enjoying.

Do we really believe that there is a Divine Energy that will take care of us and provide enough resources to take care of our needs? In Genesis 1 verse 11, God said, "Let the land produce vegetation: seed-bearing plants and trees on the land that bear fruit with seed in it, according to their various kinds. And it was so". Nature, when left on its own, provides. Masanobu Fukuoka, author of 'The One-straw Revolution' proved, for over 60 years, that after seeding abundantly with diverse, indigenous seeds and let nature take its own course, nature can and will produce enough for us without fertilizers, pesticides, herbicides or pruning. In his book, Masanobu shows, through example, that the world will sustain itself and us.

Humans don't make an acorn turn into an oak, or any other seed for that matter; nature takes care of itself. In 1 Corinthians 15, verses 37 and 38 Paul explained, "And what you put in the ground is not the plant that will grow, but only a bare seed of wheat or whatever you are planting. Then God gives it the new body he wants it to have. A different plant grows from each kind of seed." Electromagnetic energy directs and organizes the dividing cells of the seed to become the plant. If the world takes care of plants, animals, insects, and microbes then why wouldn't it take care of us?

Negative universal beliefs about the world around us will cause stress and fear. Evaluating and changing our beliefs about our world will produce huge changes in our lives. For instance, just as believing the world was flat caused people to fear falling off the world at the end of the ocean when sailing. This negative belief about the world caused unfounded fear and stress. Negative beliefs are often not in our conscience minds, but are rooted in the effects of imbedded memories. Almost all of us carry some of these negative viewpoints. Those of us that didn't receive the care and nurturing that we needed as an infant or toddler may carry more than others. Uncovering these negative attitudes and memories will make great shifts in our mental and even our physical health.

Believing that the world is able to sustain us goes a long way in easing anxiety and worry over the future. One way to see the futility of worry is to take a negative thought to the absolute worst ending. One could ask, would the world go on if I weren't on it? The answer is yes; the world would go on growing flowers and trees to feed the birds, the insects and the other animals. Now we should ask ourselves, "If I wasn't able to worry, would that change the outcome of anything; or what is the worst thing that could happen if I stopped worrying?"

We are made with craft, skill, and power to be ourselves. Scientists tell us that the first stars that were made after the singularity were comprised of only the lightest gases. It was when those stars exploded and caused nuclear fusion that heavier elements began to exist. So according to cosmologists, we are made from stardust. With each progressive species created, the world became more and more complex, and more and more diverse. The Universe loves diversity, otherwise why would it continue to become more and more diverse? Our individuality is by Divine instruction. Why would we want to be like everyone else when that is not how the Universe designed us?

Allowing ourselves the freedom to express ourselves can be difficult. Our brains are programmed to crave love and belonging as much or more than food. In fact, when baby monkeys are given the choice between a bottle of food on a wire carrier and a fur covered doll to cuddle, the babies choose the cuddling over the food. We want to be accepted. And through pain and pleasure, whether mental or physical, we grow up learning the social norms. This is good up to a point, but when all of our individuality has been programmed out of us, we forget what brings us joy and contentment. We fall out of touch with ourselves. After a while, relearning about ourselves is challenging. Sometimes it requires spending enough time alone and quiet to learn to listen internally again. It took three months of laying flat on my back, unable to get up, to begin to hear my true needs and wants. It is difficult to get past the habitual things that are chronically used to shove down the truth.

This goes for both our physical and emotional needs and wants. Once we start to listen and follow our internal directions for happiness, unhealthy craving and excessive behaviors fall away. We often use these behaviors as a way to stop experiencing our emotions. Many use food as a way to shove down emotions. Others use alcohol or drugs. Some even use chaos and bad relationships to keep from hearing their true voice. I used jogging as a way to dispel stress, which is good, but I also used it not to have to deal with conflict. Avoiding conflict is good up to a point, but when you become a doormat that others walk over rather than speaking up for yourself, jogging or any other avoidance mechanism becomes obsessive. Any behavior can be good or bad depending on how it is used and avoidance behaviors are definitely not good when they become an obsession. Exercise, because of the endorphins (self-made morphine compounds) it releases into the body, can easily be used as a way to avoid listening to ourselves and dealing with the challenges that we face. Please don't get me wrong, exercising each day is great, it is only when we use it to avoid growing and learning that it becomes a hindrance to our overall health.

Acceptance of individuality and diversity is easier when we understand that the universe creates diversity. It is what the Divine wants. In Psalms 139:14, David tells God, "Thank you for making me so wonderfully complex! Your workmanship is marvelous--how well I know it." He was aware of the complexity of our beings. He thanked God for the job that he did making him and didn't question him. Romans 9:20 asked, "But who are you, O man, to talk back to God? Shall what is formed say to him who formed it, 'Why did you make me like this?'", and Isaiah 45:9 tells us, "What sorrow awaits those who argue with their Creator. Does a clay pot argue with its maker? Does the clay dispute with the one who shapes it, saying, 'Stop, you're doing it wrong!' Does the pot exclaim, 'How clumsy can you be?" Unless we stop saying the Divine was wrong in the way we were made, we are inviting sorrow into our lives! Our complexity and individuality is made with craft and skill, with power from the Holy Spirit. Stop questioning our perfection and understand that we are perfect temples of the Holy Spirit. You are a wonderfully complex temple and arguing with your creator over that point will only create sorrow. Just think of how much distress low self-esteem causes. Embrace your individually. Be quiet and listen to what brings joy and peace to your temple.

Our individuality springs from a unified energy field. If the universe is God, it does not follow that God is the universe. Divine Energy is so much more. Isaiah wrote in chapter 45 verse 71, that God said, "I form the light, and create darkness: I make peace, and create evil: I the LORD do all these things". The Divine is everything and nothing and everything in between. The Divine is neither darkness or light, but that which exists when neither darkness nor light existed. We know this because Genesis explained it to us. In the beginning there was God, and only God. And then God created light. Divine Energy is what existed before every pair of opposites, like cold and hot or right and wrong. The Divine is the emptiness that exists around and in the opposites. Divine Space is not just the dark sky that we fly around in to get to other planets; it is that in which everything is held. Even our bodies are two thousand times more space than matter.

When we are quiet, we can find the space between thoughts and words. When we become aware of the background surrounding the physical things we recognize as solid matter, it is there that we find God. In Psalms 131:2, David tells us, "But I have stilled and quieted my soul; like a weaned child with its mother, like a weaned child is my soul within me". King David explains how safe and secure he feels when he quiets himself. When I started becoming aware of the space between the thoughts and the words that race through my mind, I began to experience the feeling that I am being supported in God. Whether through prayer, meditation or just breathing, we can sense the presence of the Divine. But more importantly, we can remember how it feels to be fully supported and safe. Not only do we house infinite energy but also we are called children of God. We are told in 1 John 2, "See what kind of love the father has given to us, that we should be called children of God; and so we are." Changing what we believe about ourselves can stop worry, anxiety and bring comfort in all social circumstances. We are as children held by our parent, just as King David described, content to feel close and to feel safe without worry or anxiety.

Judge Not Lest Ye Be Judged

While watching very young children play, I noticed that everything that they did, said, and even who they were was filtered by the fact that they were toddlers. As I watched, I found them adorable. The toddler filter that I had on in my brain didn't care if they were brown, yellow, red, black, white or purple. There was no notice of one being better looking than another, or richer, or more educated. I didn't think to myself that the kid was too fat or too skinny. I had unintentionally found a way to look at others without judging.

When we were toddlers, we didn't know what to discriminate against and when we look at toddlers we see cute, sweet babies, and don't differentiate one child as better or less than another (unless they are our own children). Going back to that three-year-old state seemed to be the way to accept others easily. Back to before we were taught to see people in defined groups. Little children are easy to love and accept even if they make mistakes. We will forgive the biggest mistakes from them, even bedwetting. That is true acceptance. In Matthew 18:3, he said: "I tell you the truth, unless you change and become like little children, you will never enter the kingdom of heaven". Of course, seeing others and ourselves without judgment is just one of the products (or fruits) of becoming like little children.

Due to our mirror neurons, special neurons that help us learn from and relate to others, when we judge others, we hold ourselves up to the same judgment. Judgment and stereotyping is learned, and like worry, it is detrimental to our self-esteem and mental health. Thinking of others and ourselves as God's toddlers is a quick way towards more positive and accepting feelings about others and ourselves. Romans 8:16 tells us that,

"The Spirit Himself testifies with our spirit that we are children of God". When we are in touch with the Holy Spirit by quieting our own spirit, we can become aware that we are all the little children of God and should be treated as such. A positive shift in beliefs and perceptions about others and ourselves reduces worry, anxiety and depression, as well as aiding in the correction of other more serious mental disorders. By changing how we perceive others, we change how we perceive ourselves.

The Bible tells us, "Judge not lest ye be judged". This means that when we judge others, we also judge ourselves. Have you ever heard the saying what goes around comes around? We reap what we sow. Newton's third law states that for every action there is an equal and opposite reaction. We all innately know that if we treat others badly we can expect to get the same in return.

Roy Mukamel, a postdoctoral fellow in Dr. Itzhak Fried's lab at UCLA, has shown that certain neurons in our brains mirror how others act and feel. Mirror neurons fire both when we watch someone doing something and when we are doing the same thing. Scientists believe that this may be a portion of how we learn empathy. The regions of our brains that are turned on may be helpful in our understanding of the emotions, intentions and actions of others. Mirror neurons may be why we can cry with the actors in movies and jump up and down, yelling, while watching players during sports. It also may be a key to how we learn so quickly by imitation. Our motor neurons can be trained by visioning ourselves doing what we have seen others do. This is why athletes envision themselves doing their important moves or plays over and over.

When we watch others being treated badly, we feel it. We learn by watching how others act and how they are responded to. I remember when I was little, watching as my father held a belt over my sister as she tried to study her timetables. Math did not come easy to her and it became even harder when our father pressured her to learn. Watching her, empathizing with her fear and pain, I learned my timetables immediately. We learn by social pressure and what we call pain and pleasure, even if it's someone else's pain or pleasure. This is why we can have such strong empathy for others. We suffer when they suffer and we learn from their suffering. Our brains fire in tandem with those around us. We learn by watching and imitating others. Paul told us in 1 Corinthians 11 verse 1, "And you should imitate me, just as I imitate Christ." Christ showed us the way to live. When we judge another or speak badly about another, our bodies know that we are projecting that same judgment on ourselves. Stop judging others and start feeling better about yourself. If we love others more and judge less, we are doing the same to ourselves. In order to stop negative self-evaluation thoughts, we must learn to stop judging others, just as we initially learned how to judge them and ourselves. In Ephesians 4 verse 4, we are told, "For there is one body and one Spirit, just as you have been called to one glorious hope for the future". We are all temples of the same Divine Spirit. Our glorious future relies on the acceptance of our unity. What we believe and think colors how we feel about everything and everyone.

I Peter 5, verses 6 and 7 told us, "Humble yourselves, therefore, under the mighty hand of God so that at the proper time he may exalt you, casting all your anxieties on him, because he cares for you". Humbling yourself just means being you! Relaxing and feeling comfortable enough about who you are to present the true you with everyone. That takes ultimate courage! Not name-dropping or having false pride is scary if you are used to using your money, degrees, or other accomplishments to build a wall between yourself and others to shield the intimate you. We are told to be our true selves, relax and let God do the worrying because we are being taken care of. If we follow the directions, little by little we can become comfortable with ourselves. Scientists tell us that social anxiety and displacement of status are associated with a thinner frontal cortex. Stress, anxiety, and depression all contribute to a brain less likely to generate new neuron and connections.

When we puff ourselves up, we are not telling the truth. It is no wonder that we start to feel more and more uncomfortable with the people around us. Trying to be someone other than who we really are is energy consuming and causes anxiety, because we are continually keeping up a lie. Ephesians 4, verse 25 said, "Therefore each of you must put off falsehood and speak truthfully to his neighbor, for we are all members of one body". Be brave enough to humble yourself and show the world your true being. This is one of the best ways to stop anxiety right in its tracks. Humbling yourself is an act of accepting that you are both strong and weak, realizing that you belong just like everyone else, just as you are.

If everyone knows who you are, there is no need to pretend how you feel, look, and think. You no longer need to compete with others. Humbling yourself can be thought about in a lot of different ways. Don't over represent yourself. An example that is very common is over spending! Mark 4, verse 19 said, "but the worries of this life, the deceitfulness of wealth and the desires for other things come in and choke the word, making it unfruitful." Lying about how much money you have causes worry. Spending on credit is lying about how much money you have. You end up wearing clothes for status and eating at expensive places that you can't afford, with people that cause discomfort. This anxiety may lead to over-eating and eating comfort foods that aren't the best choices. Choking who we really are in mountains of debt, white lies and false pretenses, is the surest way to anxiety and worry leading to chronic stress and the destruction of the health of our temples.

Finding my truth was very difficult. I believed that it was more important to be nice than to share how I really felt with others. A wise Chumash woman, named Cecilia Garcia once said that withholding the truth was not nice. She said that it was mean to send mixed messages to others because it was confusing. She told me to stop eating crow! How is that for a descriptive picture? I have stopped being pathologically nice and stopped being a doormat. At first, it was difficult to know when to say something and when not to, but the results of trying allow me to begin to like my own truths, and myself. I was forced to laugh at myself over mistakes and make candid observations of my true emotions. I was learning to become humble and honest.

Our mirror neurons help us to read other's body language, gestures and facial expressions. Autistic people's mirror neurons fail to fire when watching others. This is correlates the lack of mirror neuron firing to the inability to read other's emotions. Without this ability, our empathy for others is impeded. We wouldn't feel for others or understand what they were feeling. Our bodies tell the truth even when our mouths and our rationales don't. Through mirror neurons, our bodies tattle on us when we withhold our true feelings. Not being ourselves is lying. It sends two messages to others, one from the mouth and one from the body. Our gestures and our neurons react honestly, even if our mouths don't. Being honest means realizing what we really are; one infinite Spirit housed in diverse temples.

1 Thessalonians 4, verse 11, gave us good advice for alleviating anxiety; "Make it your ambition to lead a quiet life, to mind your own affairs, and work with your own hands, even as we charged you." We are being told to slow down,

mind our own business and work with our hands. Have you ever known anyone that seemed to thrive on drama? Everyone has met someone that can't wait to share their problems or tell you all about someone else's troubles. When gossip stirs up the community, it causes problems with everyone. Remember those mirror neurons? When you hear gossip about someone, no matter how juicy it is, you can't help but wonder if someone is talking about you. The teller, the listener and the victim all share in the negativity. This negativity causes anxiety for all concerned and costs us an efficient digestive and immune system, so mind your own business and let others mind their own life.

King Solomon wrote in Proverbs 12 verse 25, "Anxiety in a man's heart weighs it down, but a good word makes it glad". The old adage, "If you can't say something nice, don't say anything at all" protects both the parties because our mirror neurons cause us to see ourselves in others. Kind words bring peace and comfort to most situations, protecting us from anxiety and stress hormones that can cause a lack of ease or the familiar word 'disease'. Train your mind to think on whatever is true, noble, right, pure, lovely, or worthy of praise and say nice things.

Working with your hands helps to calm your mind. Hard work aids in reprogramming our neurotransmitter receptors and helps us to overcome addictive behaviors. Anything from knitting to heavy lifting will help to quiet our minds. Finding a hobby is especially important if you are one of those people that say you don't have the time. Planting a garden, making a pot or helping to build something, all retrains our brains. Try working with your hands instead of watching TV (which is mostly negative anyway), reading Facebook or Twitter, playing video games, or eating when you aren't hungry. You will quiet your head and get a sense of accomplishment if you find something you like to do.

Judgment is bad for everyone's health but how can we stop judging? We can change the structure and function of our brain by changing our beliefs. Become conscious of what you really are. Become aware of the infinite energy that we all share. I also had trouble understanding how to see the Divine in everyone. I really wanted to see spirit in everyone but I couldn't see it. Then one day, a blind friend of mine shared with me how much she disliked people trying to pray over her to heal her blindness. As far as she was concerned, she was already perfect. Suddenly, the light came on in my head; she was the perfect manifestation of infinite energy. I got it. She and everyone else, handicapped or not was perfectly made to experience the universe in a specific individual way.

This epiphany changed everything. I accepted others and myself as infinite energy that day. In 1 Corinthians 12, Paul wished that everyone were like him, but he knew that everyone has a different gift, given individually to each of us from the same Spirit. Paul understood that we are each a perfect expression of the same infinite source. In 1 Peter 4 verse 8, Peter instructed us to "Above all, love each other deeply, because love covers over a multitude of sins, purify your hearts, you double-minded". Could double-minded refer to a belief in the duality of opposites, such as them and us. Can love stop our judgment of others and ourselves? Is this why loving each other and God is so important? Could this double-mindedness be a reference to duality or always thinking in opposites? Could the parable of the garden explain the beginnings of internal stress? Was the knowledge of good and evil that we received when we ate the apple the beginning of judgment? Not God's judgment of man, but man's judgment of himself. We use our judgment to assess whether something is right or wrong, beautiful or ugly, worthy or worthless. Was this the beginning of stress? When we start to judge right and wrong in others and ourselves, we begin to feel anger and guilt. We start to feel either superior or inferior to others, which leads to pride, envy or insecurity. In the parable, we began feeling insecure and a need for material things like clothes. The story of the garden tells us that we didn't answer God's call. We began to be so lost in our own thoughts that we could no longer hear the voice of God within us. Our own thoughts of judgment and the emotions that came with them, drowned out the stillness. We were no longer in constant communication with the Divine. Stress brought changes in our epigenetic mechanisms and the diseases that follow those changes. We were no longer in the garden, illness had found its way into our temples. But the connection with the Divine is still found inside our temples. The same infinite Spirit is within each of us so judging others is merely judging ourselves, making "Judge not lest ye be judged." literally true.

Trust and Faith

Have you ever folded a piece of paper down the middle lengthwise and written down the pros and cons of a decision that you needed to make? You wrote the positive things that go along with the decision in one column and the negative outcomes in the other. You can make an informed decision using past outcomes, your experiences, or those of others. Well, that is what trust is based on, all of the outcomes or experiences. According to several Internet dictionaries, the word trust is defined as 'a confident expectation, assured reliance, or dependence on an expected outcome'. It is based on the knowledge that something will or will not occur because we have experienced it before at a prior time. A chair will hold you up. The ground will support your weight. The sun will rise in the morning. We can be assured of these things.

When we plant a seed from a seed packet, we are fairly assured that the plant named on the front of the envelope will be the one that comes up, if we take care of it according to the directions. We are sure that cats will give birth to kittens, dogs have pups, and cows have calves. Genesis tells that God determined that plants and trees produce according to their various kinds, and 1 Corinthians 15, verses 37-39 told us that plants and animals, and even men produce their like kind because God determined it. We know this is not just out of experience but also that it follows very simple rules of science. The DNA in the egg or seed dictates what is produced as an end product. DNA is constructed piece by piece and is constantly checked for quality control. It is an amazing thing that DNA and its factors self-replicates and self-regulates out almost any error! Our universe is miraculous. Einstein is quoted as saying, "There are two ways to live your life, one is as though nothing is a miracle, the other is as though everything is a miracle."

Gratitude and appreciation are the beginnings of trust. If you choose to see everything as a miracle, the fact that we can trust the air in our atmosphere to be here when we need it, or that our sun is in the sky another day makes it is easy to be grateful for nature and the earth. It is easy to see the miracle of trees giving fruit and nuts, and grass giving grain even though this earth could have been as barren as Mars or Venus. When I bite into a peach that is truly tree ripened and taste the sweetness, I can be grateful for the miracle that the flower of this tree grew parts that required pollination. I can be thankful that the bees or other insects pollinated the flower and that it grew into something so special. I can be appreciative that my taste buds can detect the sweetness and individuality of this fruit. Whether you believe in God or not, you can see the way everything works together in nature as a miracle. Remember "all things work together for those that love the Lord". This universe, the earth and the ecosphere work together to bring us everything we need.

David wrote in Psalm 52, verse 8, "But I am like an olive tree flourishing in the house of God; I trust in God's unfailing love for ever and ever". We are not expected to trust without prior experience. We can look around and be grateful for everything given to us, and know that we can trust. If we acknowledge the wonders of the universe, we are able to trust because the proof of the miraculous is all around us. The Divine Universe has proven its sustainability. All we need to do is make a list of the wonderful things around us to trust that the Divine Energy loves its creations, including us.

Broken trust colors the way we look at the universe, others and ourselves. When studying trust issues, the most extreme cases are usually looked at. Not all of us have this severity of breaches of trust, but statistics show that one in every three females has experienced some sort of sexual abuse and almost as many males. Research into cases of severely broken trust, such as found in cases of child abuse, whether in the form of physical, emotional, sexual, or neglect, shows that it affects the person's attitudes, beliefs and memories. We use these global views to appraise our experiences, others, the world, and ourselves. Our past shapes the way we trust because trust is based on our experiences. Research has shown that how we perceive or interpret the past, and not the event itself, is the most important aspect for how it affects us. Traumatized people exhibit a catastrophic way of thinking. We perceive the world as unpredictable and a disaster is always around the corner. Waiting for the other shoe to drop (so to speak), makes it extremely difficult to trust or rely on others and the world. Catastrophic thinking leads to chronic stress, anxiety, and depression. Our beliefs about ourselves modulate our self-confidence and negative beliefs can lead to social anxiety and isolation. This is why is it so important to understand that we are temples of the infinite energy field; a vehicle to house Spirit as we are expressed as individuals. We are perfectly and powerfully made to express what Spirit created. Remember, we were made by him and for him.

Of course, one doesn't have to be a victim of abuse to have trouble trusting. Neurologists and psychologists have found that neglect or a non-nurturing environment can cause some of the same effects. Witnessing violence can also cause many of the distresses seen in abuse. A young child traumatized by observing a graphic horror or slasher movie may carry that memory and younger children may react to situations as if abused by expressing fear, anxiety and always being on edge. Most of us can remember having nightmares over a scary movie that we watched just before going to bed. Violent television takes its toll on our bodies and or minds especially if one perceives the presented violence as a true threat. Our negative and fear based newscasts also push our minds into a fear-based thought pattern. If a child is abused, neglected or a witness to violence, an inability to talk about the issue or tell the truth is often due to shame, guilt, or freezing (as seen in fight, flight or free). It can lead to avoidance behavior springing from anxiety, or fear of loss and abandonment. Trying to self-heal or self-medicate can be one reason for drug and alcohol abuse, as well as obesity. The development of substance abuse, obesity, and anxiety is common in people with trust issues. Sleep disorders such as insomnia and nightmares are also common. Having and maintaining trust is extremely important to living a healthy and happy life free from stress.

Trust is a key element in reducing anxiety and worry. Learning to trust requires changing our beliefs, assumptions, and how we perceive our memories. Getting to know our true assumptions and beliefs can be difficult because we carry many of them subconsciously. Sometimes finding a supportive environment while play-acting, painting, drawing and sculpting can help us to understand what assumptions and beliefs we carry. Understanding them will help us to change them. We can engage an active imaginative and creative process to promote healing responses, and bridges conscious and unconscious thought processes. Understanding of our subconscious beliefs can come though art, music, dance or some kind of positive self-expression.

Other multi-sensory or enriched environments provide a safe environment to gain trust. Traumatic memories are often stored together with situational cues that are linked to our senses. Pavlov and Skinner believed that conditioning is important to behavior. By repeatedly pairing trauma with neutral cues, we are conditioned to produce anxiety and fear. This also may be true for a one-time event that was exceedingly shocking and not something that we can premeditate. An example of this would be a horn wailing (the neutral cue) just before a car wreck (the trauma). In order for the conditioning to be undone, the neutral cue must be repeatedly presented without the trauma in a safe nurturing environment. Multi-sensory experiences or enriched environments help to rewrite the cues that cause memories to surface. MRI scans and other results have shown that enriched environments not only induce the production of new neurons but also aid in the growth of brain structures like the hippocampus and cortex. Reducing stress responses help to protect the new cells and allow more to mature. The more senses we incorporate, and the more joy we experience, the more improvements we make to our brains. We all have the ability to learn new more effective behaviors and grow new neurons. Boosting the birth of new neurons, called neuroneogenesis, in the hippocampus, enhances our ability to recognize patterns, which helps us to locate ourselves in space and time. When we are lost, even for a minute, we can feel anxious. A healthy hippocampus can keep us from feeling lost. Environmental enrichment and exercise can stimulate neuroneogenesis. Exercise has the added natural effect of improving mood and alleviating anxiety and depression.

Nurturing safe relationships and social networks are a fundamental part of learning trust. Scanning of the hippocampus of neglected and normal children age 3-7 has revealed that nurturing has a huge impact on the size of the hippocampus. The hippocampus is the part of the brain that is involved in our stress response, memory, and learning. The researchers tested the parent's response to the child during the completing of a stressful task. The more able the parent is to nurture, the larger the hippocampus of the child, up to 10% larger. Greater fear, which translates into less trust, is associated with a larger amygdala and a smaller the hippocampus. Nurturing impacts our nervous system and impacts brain development. An enlarged amygdala is associated with more fear responses.

Chronic fear is related to hormonal changes including elevated cortisol levels and reduced growth hormone. It impairs cognitive brain function and growth. These impacts can make us less able to modulate our emotions in proportion to what the situation calls for causing us to over-react. We can also re-create trauma repetitively. 'Drama, drama, drama', we surround ourselves with people and situations that prove over and over to us that the world and others can't be trusted. This can lead to depression, anxiety, and behavioral problems.

Our perceptions, or how we view the world are paramount but we can change them. We can use art, music, dance or other creative outlets to release our negative emotions. In Psalms 59, verse 16, David said, "But I will sing of your strength, in the morning I will sing of your love; for you are my fortress, my refuge in times of trouble". Singing positive affirmations is a great way to re-teach ourselves and rewire our brains. Music works on both the conscious and subconscious mind. Research into the effects of music on stress has shown a significant reduction depending on the type of music, age, type of stress and what techniques are being used with the music. Positive affirmations and gratitude have been found to improve self-confidence and reduce negative self-talk. Negative self-talk are those damaging tapes we play in our minds.

Positive peer group, social and family support can decrease the negative effects that cause lack of trust. As we have seen, by using our mirror cells, people learn by observing and imitating others. We all have the ability to learn new more effective behaviors. Observation of live model or mentor or connecting to an imaginary hero that is coping with fear and copying them, helps us to practice life skills. Role-playing, storytelling and communicating with a nurturing caregiver or mentor, helps us to relearn correct beliefs. Our environment and our interpersonal relationships shape the functioning of our genetic traits. Neglect and abuse at an early age causes epigenetic changes that can predispose us to anxiety, depression, suicide and addiction. Proper nutrition and safe environments filled with enjoyable, multi-sensory activities can enable our brains and our genetic expression to be corrected. This is how our environment pressures our epigenetic structure to adapt.

Story-telling is used for processing the past and initiating a new narrative. We all create a personal fable or narrative about our past that leads us to our beliefs and attitudes. These attitudes, beliefs and memories are important in how we appraise our experiences, others, the world and ourselves. If we rebuild and re-order how we see the universe, others and ourselves, we can build trust. Sometimes it is important to construct a new narrative. This is giving the past a different meaning. This is helpful to stop trying to undo the past by asking, "why did it happen or what if". Trust requires action, so changing behaviors is required along with managing emotions. Wayne Dyer wrote an example of a new narrative or life story in his book, *Heal your Life*. The narrative helped him forgive his father, who repeatedly abused him. Dr. Dyer chose to believe that his father volunteered to come to earth and act like a monster so that Wayne could learn to forgive. Wayne chose to believe that being a monster is a huge sacrifice because abusers are hated and despised. With this narrative or story, he then could be grateful to his father for teaching him. Wayne didn't need to forgive his father because there was nothing to forgive and his abuse was given a reason. Sometimes use giving the past a reason or purpose changes everything.

This story may not work for you but you can find one that does. Maybe it is as simple as really putting yourself in the other person's body. What would you feel if you grew up and lived the same life as that person? Repeatedly telling the new narrative, including an acknowledgement of the negative, serves to desensitize and strengthen a new way of viewing life. Repetition stops the fear mechanism and disrupts the emotional cycle of anxiety and depression. A new personal view of the past through story telling, challenges and changes beliefs and assumptions.

Trust is a choice. It begins when we decide we want to have a close relationship with someone whether it is a friend, partner or relative. To trust, we must know who we are and be strong enough to stand up for ourselves. We are the temples that hold the light of the world. Intimacy can only start when we know ourselves. Being in a real relationship requires that both parties show who they really are to each other and not just what you think the other person wants to see. Be truly yourself and trust that your anxieties will be taken care of one way or another. Do you believe that all things work together? Do you understand that physics tells us that we are made of infinite energy and by infinite energy?

What does trust feel like? When one trusts, you feel confident. With this confidence comes the absence of worry. Trust is built on a track record, a consistent, honest follow-through or integrity. Trust can also grow stronger if through open, honest communication, both parties have the opportunity to correct mistakes and try again. Being true to one's self requires telling the truth, even when it is unpleasant, doesn't make you look good, and can cause conflict. Don't pretend to be someone else. Don't throw truth away to protect the other person from upset; it is dishonest. We can trust others to love what and who we truly are.

In Matthew 6, verse 34, Jesus said; "So don't be anxious about tomorrow. God will take care of your tomorrow too. Live one day at a time." Live now, not in the past or the future! That means take a deep breath, stop the conversation you are having in your head with yourself, and take a look around. Use your senses. Listen to the birds, crickets and other noises that are happening right now. Notice the colors and smells in the area. Touch the green grass with your bare feet. Become aware of all of your senses just by quieting your thoughts. This is the type of multi-sensory or enriched environment therapy that will enhance the growth of new neurons in your brain.

Have you ever been so caught up in your own thoughts that you pass the street that you wanted to turn on? And, when you come out of your thoughts, all of a sudden you notice everything around you? That instance is living in the now. You are aware in that instance of the present moment. Living in the moment is quieting your brain and sensing everything. No internal thoughts, just noticing what is happening at this moment.

Living today also means avoiding rehashing the past and worrying about the future. Rerunning tapes of the past only causes your body to re-live stresses that aren't happening. All negative emotions affect our physical and mental health even if we are just replaying past negative emotions. The body doesn't understand time. It perceives the re-hashing of past stresses as present stress and sends hormones to prepare us for fight or flight. That is why it is so important to let go of past fears, anger, regrets and guilt. The Bible already contained this information over 2000 years ago. "Live one day at a time."

Living today means letting go of the past. Don't live each day as if the past will affect the future. All of us have had bad things happen. We have done things that we are not proud of in the past. Do you assume that you will be treated the same way as in the past? Letting go of past mistakes frees your life up to be lived to day, new.

Being anxious about the future is not any better. The emotions still affect the body whether the emotions are real or just perceived. Don't waste your health and energy on things that aren't happening right this moment! Remember, The Divine has already taken care of tomorrow; all you have to do is live in faith, one day at a time.

Philippians 4, verse 6 told us, "Do not be anxious about anything, but in everything, by prayer and petition, with Thanksgiving, present your requests to God. And the peace of God, which transcends all understanding, will guard your hearts and your minds in Christ Jesus." 'With thanksgiving' means to ask God as if it is already done. Present your worries to God with the faith that the outcome is good even if you can't understand how it is going to happen. Do this for everything, all of the time, every day. Faith and trust are different. Trust is compiling a list of the positive things that have already happened to build a basis for believing. Biophysics is helping us to build this foundation.

Faith is different than trust. When we trust in a Divine Universe, we do it based on the good things that go on around us every day. Developing trust in anything is as easy as starting a list of the positive things that person or thing has done. Will water run from the faucet when I turn it on? It will run if someone has paid the bill. Now, that's where we can get into faith. Faith is a belief that is not based on proof. Trust is believing a parent will pay your water bill because in the past it has always been paid. Faith is believing in something when we have no previous experience or proof that it is true, and acting on that belief. It transcends our understanding. Faith requires something from us. We must take an action without prior proof of the result. The saying 'Just do it!' is the essence of faith, belief with action. Don't think about it, just jump in. Faith requires that we take an action and believe without the assurance that the right outcome will occur. This is why we hear that 'faith without works is dead'. Without action, faith is merely a hope with no confidence powering it.

James 2, verses 15-24 told us that faith without works doesn't mean anything. There is no proof of faith if there is no action. It is not that we have to work to please the Divine. It is through acting and seeing the results that we turn hope into trust. In Romans 15:13, Paul says," I pray that God, the source of hope, will fill you completely with joy and peace because you trust in him. Then you will overflow with confident hope through the power of the Holy Spirit". Turning hope or faith into trust fills us with joy and peace.

Faith has been shown clinically to help people to improve their healing. This is seen in the form of a sudden miracle, finding a new purpose in life, or connecting with a network for intercessory prayer and continued aid. A study of women associated by a faith-based organization found that the women increased the amount of exercise and lowered their blood pressure better than women not united in faith. Being in a faith-based community can heal you just by holding each other up with mentors, prayer, and communication during hard times.

Faith makes it possible to achieve the changes necessary to restore the temple for the Holy Spirit. In Mark 9, verse 23, Jesus said, "Everything is possible for him who believes." Don't ask if you can, everything is possible! James 5, verse 15 said, "and the prayer offered in faith will restore the one who is sick" Why does faith work? James told us in chapter1, verse 6, "But when he asks, he must believe and not doubt, because he who doubts is like a wave of the sea, blown and tossed by the wind". Electromagnetic fields leave our bodies to interact with the infinite energy field. Energy fields leave our brains and hearts too. Photon light is emitted from our bodies. Remember that everything is a wave from the electromagnetic sea known as zero-point energy. Scientists can measure the negative electromagnetic fields that tell cells how to heal. Disruption of these fields can stop healing and even halt the regeneration of an amphibian's limb. Many people believe that these electromagnetic fields are how our faith affects healing and interacts with the universal energy field.

Does the emotion of true faith really change the chemistry of our bodies? We have all heard of the placebo effect but did you know the nocebo effect is just as effective? Christ told us over and over that "As you believe so shall it be done to you", and "According to your faith will it be done to you". Healing can take many forms. Whether it is a physical healing, a mental healing, or an emotional healing, healing has been promised according to the faith we have. Science calls this type of healing the placebo effect, and double blind studies have proven the benefits of sugar pills and a positive diagnosis. There is also a documented nocebo effect, which demonstrates the opposite of the positive effects of a placebo. This happens if there is a mention of a negative outcome or side effect accompanying an illness or treatment. These negative outcomes can range from acid stomach from a pill, to a mistaken diagnosis leading to the un-indicated death of an individual.

If one believes that bad will happen, it probably will. Placebo and nocebo effects are associated with opposite responses of our dopamine system, and our endorphin or natural opium systems. These systems are located in the same areas of our brains that involve our reward responses and motivate behavior. They seem to overlap with our emotional brain regions. These natural systems may over-ride our stress systems and help our bodies to heal. Christ understood this

2000 years ago. So why is it so important to trust and have faith? Over and over the scriptures tell us "your faith has healed you". Trust teaches us to see the world without fear to shut off stress hormones and faith turns on the healing powers of the body.

Forgiveness

We can cause permanent changes in our lives by shifting our perceptions about how others treat us. We can view our problems in a new light. Actually understanding "what is that good, and acceptable, and perfect, will of God" could be simply taking literally the written words in the Bible. Words like "Father, forgive them; for they know not what they do" gives us a view not only of what we need to do when others treat us badly, but also how to do it. A change in how we perceive the wrong doing of another is the most significant shift we can make in forgiving someone. How we view the offence is more important than the actual wrongdoing. Our perceptions are the only things that matter to our bodies.

Holding grudges, anger, and resentment destroys our health. Christ's words, at Calvary, demonstrate his perception of the wrongdoings of the people that tortured and crucified him. He chose to see them as not knowing or understanding what they were doing. He showed us how to set ourselves free from resentment and rage. By believing that they didn't understand, Jesus truly loosened the chains of blame and freed himself from any negative emotions. Remember, what we perceive as happening is the most important thing! Renewing our minds leads to emotional and physical health.

We see many places in the Bible with the same message as Colossians 3, verse 13, "Bear with each other and forgive whatever grievances you may have against one another. Forgive as the Lord forgave you". Why is it so important to be patient with each other and not hold grudges? Constantly, holding on to past regrets and anger is like handing your Divine Energy over to the person or event that hurt or angered you. The cost is too high! It leads to depression. Don't hang on to bad feelings. In Proverbs 15, verse 13, we are told to have a happy heart and a smile. They will reflect your spirit. We are only victims to past transgressions done against us as long as we make others responsible for our unhappiness. Release the past!

In the Bible, forgiveness and healing always go hand in hand. Christ says; "your sins are forgiven, you are healed" and blind see, lame walk, and chronic diseases disappear. In Psalm 103 verse 3, David told us, "He forgives all my sins and heals ALL my Diseases." Why is it so important to forgive in order to heal? Ridding our bodies of negative emotions go hand in hand with healing them.

Remember, our neurons convert our thoughts and emotions into energy and chemicals that direct our bodies. What we see, hear, taste, smell, touch and feel are all transmitted into our bodies through our central nervous system. Our emotional or limbic brain includes parts of our frontal cortex. The cortex is the thinking cap that is worn on the very outermost part of our brains. This is the part of the brain that regulates our social behaviors and helps us to delay gratification. Fueled by dopamine as a reward, our frontal cortex helps to drive hard for our goals and dreams. Our cortex helps to organize our thoughts, remembers the rules of our tasks, and directs us to follow our moral values. Our frontal cortex develops last, usually by age 25. This may be why teenagers often make questionable decisions. Our cortex helps us to modulate our emotions and reactions, and is very changeable. It is the part of the brain that is least regulated by our genes and most influenced by our environments. This is really great news! This is the part of our brains that we can use to change our reactions and emotions towards others. So, we can train it to be less reactive, less judgmental, and less angry. Our transformable cortex gives us the ability to change how we think and modify our health.

Unfortunately, our frontal cortex is also extremely fragile. Glucocorticoids or stress hormones kill neurons in the cortex of our brains. Chronic stress shrinks the size of the cortex making it harder to control our emotions. Anger and resentment cause the amygdala, the part of the limbic brain that activates mostly due to fear, to send a spike or action potential to a signaling center called the hypothalamus. The hypothalamus shoots the stress signal to the pituitary, which tells the adrenal glands to release stress hormones like adrenaline and cortisol. This is how the fight or flight mechanism works.

This is all fine and dandy if we are running for our life from a gang-banger with a gun, but not if we are rehashing something that happened several days or even years before. The stress hormones are supposed to give us the energy to run or kick. They direct our glucose to our thigh muscles, our brains, and to our lungs. This is great in the short run. But, if we don't use up the hormones by running or fighting, or if we continue to fume and rage about the negative things that have happened, the stress hormones deplete our cortex of glucose and change the regulation of our neuropeptides and their receptors. This can kill neurons, stop the birth and maturing of new neurons, and leave us open to anxiety and bad decisions.

How can we let go of the past and forgive? Well, first let's look at the costs if we don't. Continued negative thoughts drain the emotional vitality that God promises us. Loss of this energy leads to chronic depression and fatigue, and ultimately sickness. This happens when negative emotions consistently send signals to the central nervous system saying that you are suffering a loss or fear of loss. Fear signals a cascade of hormones that shut down our digestive system and our immune system to reroute energy, in order to fight off this loss that our body perceives as a threat to our existence. Continued negative thoughts and emotions keep the hormones high. This lowers our ability to nourish our body and keep our immune system mobilized properly. It gives the persons or things that we believe to have hurt us the power to continue hurting us. Take back the power that God has given you!

Forgiveness is selfish! It takes back your power. In Mark 11, verse 25, God promised that if we forgive, God *will* forgive. That lightness that you feel when you have forgiven or been given forgiveness is Divine energy running freely through you again. Forgiveness halts the stress hormones that inhibit the energy flow to the parts of your body that are needed to maintain vital health. If our bodies have low immunity and nourishment, we are inviting viruses, bacteria, and fungi to overcome us. Continued negative emotions and concurrent low energy may lead to chronic illness. Forgiveness is one of the steps to health, vitality; and the promised energy or power the Bible tells us about.

How Does One Forgive and Let Go of the Past?

Matthew told us in chapter 5, verse 44, to pray for and to love our enemies, and Paul told us in Romans 12, verse 20 to feed them. In verse 21, we are told that we can overcome evil with good. Pray for the people that hurt you like you would a small child that has done something harmful. Don't attach negative thoughts about why they did the action. All negative feelings begin with fear, fear of loss of something. This could be a fear of the loss of love, respect, life, body, and material things like money, etcetera. A fear of loss may, of course feel real, but we are promised in 1 John 4, verse 18, that perfect love casts out fear. Remember, all things of this world pass away. Don't fear the loss of things that aren't really worth attaching to. Of course this doesn't mean if someone is trying to physically harm you, your child or someone else, that you shouldn't react, only that you shouldn't attach to the memory of it.

Fear is passed from fathers to their offspring through the epigenetic binding of methyl groups to DNA. The epigenetic changes sensitize children to the thing that the father is afraid of. If a father is afraid of the smell of a bear, it is important that a child have enhanced awareness of the scent of a bear. But if the father is fearful of loss of something less dangerous and he spends his time worrying about it, his child may also be epigenetically predisposed to fear that specific thing. Do we want our children to share our fears, remembering that out of fear springs hatred and judgment?

In Psalm 27, verse 1, David wrote: "The Lord is my light and salvation, whom shall I fear?" The light energy of the Divine forms us and believing saves us from fear. The bottom line is that what we truly believe changes, not just what we fear, but also our entire perception. Without fear, we act without anger or high emotions. Science today points to an infinite source, one that we can choose to call God. The more we learn about zero-point energy or the energy of the vacuum, the easier it is to believe in one universal God. What we believe changes everything.

How does one love perfectly the enemies that have tried to harm you? Stop reliving the act in your head. Go on a negative energy fast. Yell, "stop" as loud as you can, or smile and raise your eyebrows and arms up as high as you can. Our body language changes our emotions. These simple acts throw a wrench into the trauma mechanism and stop the pit bull-like circular thinking, enabling us to let go of the past.

Try to rewrite the negative experience in a way that allows for you to have perceived it incorrectly. Often, we are angry about something that has happened in the past. If the incident happened when you were three, you are letting a three-year-old dictate how you feel today! When I realized that my perspective was based on a toddler's view of life, I decided to rewrite my story. It doesn't matter if the story is the absolute factual way it happened, only that it is your perspective on what happened. If you ask five witnesses to describe an accident, you will get five different perspectives. Everyone sees things from their own vantage point, shaded with colors of the their past and their beliefs. Just like Jesus deciding to see the Roman soldiers as not understanding, we can change how we look at others and the things they do.

I heard a story about a husband and a wife. The wife made the husband toast with his breakfast each morning and each morning the husband got more and more upset. The high emotions were affecting their whole marriage. Finally, one morning the husband slammed his hand down on the table when she served him breakfast and yelled, "Why do you always give me the crusted ends of the bread? Don't you respect the way I work and pay for the food? Don't you love me or think enough of me to give me the good parts of the bread?" The wife astonished but relieved by his outbreak responded, "I give you the crusty ends of the bread because they are my favorite. I didn't know you didn't like them. I won't give them to you anymore."

I love this story because I love the crusty ends of the bread and so do my kids, and they always give them to me. The important thing to take from this story is that we don't always know why a person acts the way they do. Was the action a cry for help? Was it done out of fear also? Was it done from a place of immaturity or stupidity? Is it worth you giving them your health and power? Like Jesus, ask yourself if they knew what they were doing. Change your perception of the malice involved and give others the benefit of the doubt. When you pray to forgive, picture the person as a hurt child. Pick the child up and place your hand over their hurt part and pray for God to heal them. Feel the love that a mother would feel when praying over their hurt toddler. That is perfect love. This is what the act of feeding them does. It helps us to see them as needy and human. Remember that forgiveness is a selfish act that may save you from coronary heart disease, metabolic syndrome, eating disorders, and road accidents.

Chronic anger or hostility acts to instigate a cycle in our emotional center, called the amygdala, which causes the hypothalamus to release two important peptides. These peptides stimulate the pituitary gland, which is located just below the hypothalamus to secrete a hormone that travels down to the adrenal glands sitting above the kidneys. This hormone, known as adrenocorticotropic hormone or corticotropin, initiates the production of glucocorticoids. The main glucocorticoid hormone is called cortisol. This is the same hormone that response to stress or fear, and sends your body into fight or flight mode. It suppresses your digestion and immunity, in order to give the blood supply to the parts of your body needed to fight or run.

Staying in this mode too long, like when you are resentful, hold a grudge or harbor hatred, causes cortisol to counteract insulin to contribute to insulin resistance, chronic fatigue, insomnia, and memory and cognitive problems. Chronically increased levels of cortisol induce collagen loss leaving your skin looking and feeling older and more wrinkled. It also inhibits immunoglobulin A, which is an antibody that protects your mucous membranes from invasion. Without this protection, each opening your body has to the outside is vulnerable to attack. This includes your eyes, nose, mouth, genitourinary tract, gastrointestinal tract, prostate, and respiratory system. Wow, that means that the grudge you haven't forgiven will make you look old and fat. Oh, and girls, you know that yeast inflection that you can't seem to get rid of? Forgiveness may help. And men, that person that you continually want to punch could be affecting your prostate and sex life. You tell me, is it worth the lingering thoughts of revenge? Do yourself a favor, forgive and forget. Change the way you see the other person and give yourself a break.

Uncover your buried negative feelings associated with an incident, and admit to fear, anger and or other negative emotions. This doesn't mean that you have to remember everything that happened, only the emotions. Recognize that you are hurt, angry, hateful, fearful, or resentful. Admit that you have them. We want to be good people, but being a good person doesn't mean never acknowledging feelings of hurt, anger, or hatred. Ephesians 4, verse 26 reminded us to "never let the sun set on our anger", it doesn't tell us to pretend it isn't there.

Realize that only you can control and change your emotions. You are no longer a victim when your take back the control over your own emotions. Our frontal cortex (the outside membrane of our brain) can be used to regulate the harder more desirable actions. Our frontal cortex is closely connected to the parts of our brain that regulate our emotions and our reward system. Dopamine is the fuel that drives our striving to regulate social behavior, and reach goals. It enables us to do the right thing, even if it's harder than doing the wrong thing. Our cortex and dopamine are the reasons that we can delay gratification and feel great when we reach our goals. Cortical neurons are connected throughout the brain, and they are very active and fragile. We can use our frontal cortex to unlearn our fears and reactions to the environmental stimuli that cause us continuous stress or anxiety.

How can we recondition our reactions? We make a rule and follow it, over and over. For instance, if the rule is that we do something nice every time we feel negatively towards a person and then we do something nice every time, we habituate the reaction. We must do something positive. If we decide that we aren't going to react with a negative feeling towards someone that is rude or unfriendly towards us, it won't work as well. We must habituate positive actions and emotions; and not doing something isn't as affective. When these positive habits become automatic, they are ruled over by a different part of the brain and the stimulus no longer makes us angry, fearful, or any other negative feeling. I am not saying that there is no time in which you can legitimately rise to anger or fear, only that we don't need to be ruled by it. We don't need to live in chronic stress, anger, or anxiety. I try to do something nice for my husband every time we have a fight, even if I don't feel like it. I usually go purchase something small that he needs like socks or t-shirts. It helps to mitigate some of my negative emotions. I must practice these things or I end up ruminating about the fight (big or small) night and day. This is how I try to never go to bed angry.

The ability of our frontal cortex to reign over our emotions is one of the last things to develop in our brains. This is why teenagers and young adults still have problems with moral decisions and behavioral controls. To be fully in control of one's emotions is a sign of a mature adult. Learned environmental stimuli and not our genes rule the frontal cortex. The Bible's instructions help us to learn correct responses to become people that are ruled by our love and compassion and not by anger and fear. This may be why the Bible repeatedly directs us to love. In 1 John 4, verses 16 and 18, it is written that God is love and if we love, God lives in us and we in him. There is no fear in love because love casts out fear. Positive emotions allow infinite energy to flow throughout our bodies, our temples.

Our frontal cortex reigns over our animalistic reactions such as aggression. Learned behaviors control our frontal cortex and we can re-train it with love. Health can begin only after one forgives. Dr. Robert Enright has done many years of research on forgiveness and hostility. He believes that forgiveness is self-love. His research demonstrates that forgiveness decreases depression and anxiety, while increasing well-being, hope, and social interactions. His studies include incest survivors, victims of violent crimes and domestic violence, and people of all ages. His research reveals a decrease in heart and vascular problems when one lowers anger and hostility. Psalms says, "An anxious heart weighs a man down, but a kind word cheers him up".

Commit to forgiving, for your own health and happiness. Decide to free yourself. This does not depend on whether the offender is sorry or not. Accept that you feel undeserved pain from the action of the offender, but choose not to pass on any negativity. In other words, acknowledge that what happened wasn't your fault but choose to be responsible for what you think, feel and do, in spite of the injury and the offender. Proverbs 17, verse 22 said; "A cheerful heart is good medicine, but a crushed spirit dries up the bones". Science agrees, persistent negative emotions can lead to chronic illness.

Rewrite the injury in a completely new context. This may mean seeing the abuser as an abused child or maybe as a monster that helped you to develop into the amazing person you are. Remember how Christ saw his abusers, as if they didn't fully realize what they were doing. Maybe they were just following orders, or they didn't know who he was and truly believed that he was a criminal. The idea is to put a 'maybe' into how you look at the offender or the incident. Any way you choose to rewrite it to release blame is acceptable. It merely means that you are filled with positive, life giving emotions. Have compassion for the enemies. Chose to let go of the need for retribution. This empties your body of the repercussions of negative emotions that cause stress, anxiety, depression and illness. It allows you to grow into a better, more emotionally controlled person. This helps develop self-esteem and feelings of emotional well-being.

Put a purpose on the incident, always looking for a greater good and giving the abuse incident a purpose. Remember Paul wrote in Romans 8, verse 28 that "all things work together for the good of those that love the Lord". Believe that universal energy is really interacting with you, hearing your heart and your mind. This doesn't mean you condone the action or need to reconcile. Find a reason for the suffering. It may make you more understanding and compassionate to others going through similar situations, and to yourself. You may develop a new openness and acceptance to others that manifests itself in new, deeper relationships, which increase social interaction and lowers anxiety, loneliness, and depression. Forgiveness makes you stronger not weaker. When you give forgiveness you gain much more than you give away.

Imaging by FMRI has shown that negative self-beliefs cause the same firing of neurons in the amygdala as being angry or fearful. The Bible gives us many instructions to counteract these negative self-beliefs. First and foremost, we need to understand that we are all temples and are made from the energy of the Divine. This means everyone. No one is better or worse. In the past, I have asked myself how this could be true. How can a murderer be no worse than a nun that has given herself fully to the service of others? The answer is simply to see everything as made from the perfect energy of the Divine. Our worth is not based on what we do but what we are. We are temples that are made in the image of God. No judgment and no casting of stones at others or ourselves. When we understand this truly, we can see who we are and change the beliefs and assumptions that we hold about others and ourselves. We can finally be free of shame and guilt, as well as resentment, anger and a need for revenge.

Forgiving and non-judgment is the beginning of our recovery! Clearing the negative thoughts about others and ourselves stops our fight or flight mechanisms. It allows the redirection of blood and energy to return balance to our bodies. The link between self-judgment and the judgment of others is astounding. When we begin to recognize that we are all beings made from the Spirit energy of God, we stop looking at what we do and automatically start to heal. Being, not doing, makes us who we are at our core.

Forgiving ourselves is also important. Love yourself no matter what has happened. Tell yourself you are sorry and ask to forgive yourself. Admit your responsibility, but still feel the forgiveness. Realize that you are accepting things as they are right now at this precise moment. Now tell yourself, "thank you" for the forgiveness. Love, acceptance, and gratitude are emotions that return well-being to our bodies and minds.

Asking forgiveness from others may be an important part of forgiving ourselves, and releasing guilt and other negative feelings about ourselves. Some people have trouble with apologies. Psychologists say that the easiest way to apologize is to do it as soon as possible. When speaking to the person you have wronged, describe the specific incident or behavior. Explain how unloving, cruel, thoughtless, or stupidly you acted. Be honest and sincere. Acknowledge that your behavior was unacceptable and promise that it will not happen again. Think of a way to make it up to them. Then ask them to accept your apology.

Now, stand there and listen without interrupting. Don't defend yourself! Hear their hurt and anger. No matter if the person accepts your apology or not, forgive yourself and acknowledge any growth that has occurred. Forgiving yourself does not depend on whether others forgive you.

Letting go of the past may also mean letting go of negative assumptions and beliefs. If you grew up believing that you have to make your money, get married, or reach a certain benchmark in your career before a certain age, your birthday each year may give you negative emotions. You can rewrite those beliefs by concentrating on being grateful for the things in your life today. It sounds too simple but self-regulation is a proven way of changing your brain patterns. Just believing that infinite energy interacts with each of us empowers us to change how we perceive the world and ourselves. If we change our beliefs and assumptions, we change our physical bodies and the way we see the world.

Many people believe that testosterone causes a person to be aggressive or hot tempered. Science has shown that this is not true. The feelings that are already present drive the testosterone. It only increases anger and aggression if anger is already turned on by the amygdala and the sympathetic nervous system is aroused. In other words, if the stimulus activates the amygdala, testosterone ramps the reaction and amplifies existing behaviors. Testosterone should not be used as an excuse not to regulate your emotions. Realize that each of us is in control of our own feelings and reactions.

Science tells us that we really only have two emotions: love and fear, and everything else is just a shade of one or the other. We are told that God is love, love comes from God, and that if we love, we live in God, and he in us. Tapping into love maintains vital energy flow within our bodies allowing all our organ systems access to blood, nutrients, oxygen and immune factors.. This energy transfer maintains our bodies, and without it, life is not possible. True love gets rid of fear! Love crowds out all the negative emotions that cause stress hormones. Fall in love with something. Fall in love with being in love. When you focus on something, you begin to see it everywhere. If you love red roses or shiny Harley Davidsons and start to look for them, you begin to notice them all of the time. When you are focused on what you love, time flies and everything else falls away. Love squeezes out fear. It actually retrains our brains fear responses. Jesus said, "Forgive them, for they know not what they do". He separated the person from the event. His perception was that they didn't understand and were possibly merely following orders. He still loved them but not the deed. The event had a purpose! Find your own purpose, forgive and love because forgiveness and healing can't be separated.

Ending Fear with Compassion

Many people's minds get caught in endless loops of negative emotions, which the amygdala receives as fear. They are constantly reliving arguments and other incidents. These loops rerun the incident to figure it out and rationalize it, over and over and over. This kind of thinking never works. (I know because I was one of these people. For years, if I had an argument or an incident, I couldn't sleep or even think clearly.) Albert Einstein is quoted as saying, "You can never solve a problem on the level on which it was created".

This repetitive thinking affects our ability to work, play, and even communicate with other people. For some people, if there is an argument, they can't enjoy going out to dinner with friends till the fight is cleared up. Many people can't sleep while rerunning their experiences. This drives the people close to them crazy, because others don't always need to talk an argument into the ground to stop their heads. This kind of perpetual negative thinking is harmful to our moods and can lead to chronic anxiety and depression. Why some people are more anxious and can't seem to let go could largely be from environmental and epigenetic effects. The wiring of our neural circuitry is linked to how well we were nurtured as little ones, as well as social community feedbacks. The more stress and the less nurturing we received as infants, the bigger the wiring problem. Thankfully, our wiring isn't completely permanent.

Our brains, hearts and alimentary tracts (Gut: the tube that sends food to body) all have inputs into our emotional health. Both the Gut and the heart relay messages to the brain via the vagus nerve. Our hearts and Guts transmit messages of emotions. Amazingly, most of our serotonin, the neurotransmitter that tells us that everything is good, is housed in our Guts and not in our brains.

The writers of the Bible knew that our hearts and Guts were the seat of our emotions. In Psalm 28, verse 7, David's "heart leaps for joy". Conversely, in Jeremiah 4, verse 19, Jeremiah told us of the pain in the pit of his stomach or bowels and the "agony of his heart pounding within him". In Proverbs 15, verse 13, we are told, "a happy heart makes a happy face but heartache crushes the spirit". The Webster's Unabridged Dictionary defines the heart not only as an organ but also as the seat of the affections or sensibilities. Our hearts leap for joy, pound in fear, hold us steady, and can change how we look and our outward expressions.

Psychologists like Stephen Porges measure the variation in heart rates. When heart rate variability is measured in infants and adults, it reveals that variability increases due to positive social interactions and positive emotions such as happiness, awe, gratitude and love. According to Scientific America in Oct. 2010, the ability to modulate your own heart rate demonstrates a capacity for social sensitivity and an increase in social skills. Learning to regulate our heartbeat helps us cope with stress, emotions, and decision-making.

Studies of meditation concentrating on loving kindness have demonstrated an improvement in the tone of the vagus nerve. Vagal tone stimulation reduces heart failure, restores balance within our nervous system, and is associated with well-being. Imaging studies show that compassionate mediation or prayer increases our ability to stop our mood swings. It also decreases the constant conversations in our heads and negative self-talk by quieting the emotional areas of our brains. Mindfulness means to remember or to pay attention to a thought or emotion. Mindful compassion training can positively rewire our brains to decrease anxiety or fear. At Havard Medical School, Dr. Gaelle Desbordes and his colleages revealed through brain imaging, that if compassionate meditation is practiced regularly, structural changes enable our brains to heal from anxiety or learned chronic fear. These studies have shown decreases in negative emotions and reduced amygdala activity, which is our area of fear response. The participants exhibited less emotional reactivity and enhanced ability for emotional regulation. They also reported less anxiety, depression and higher self-esteem, all by practicing focused breathing, meditation or prayer. Daily practicing of compassionate meditation has shown to reduce stress, enhance immunity, and lower fatigue, depression, anxiety and anger. Maybe this is what the Bible meant when we were told that there is no fear in love. Imaging has shown that compassionate meditation or prayer done six days a week for only thirty minutes per day, will start to induce these changes in our brain wiring in only eight weeks.

Awareness of suffering and a deep desire to stop the pain in others is what is called compassion. One way of starting a practice of a mind full of compassion is to sit quietly thinking compassionately about a person that you love. I chose a time in my life when my daughters' were very ill. I meditated on the feelings of love I had for them and how much I wanted to help them to heal. Most of us can remember picking up a child that has just fallen. We pick them up, hold and rock them, say soothing things, kiss the 'ouch', and place a bandage or ice on it. We are able to focus on a person that we love and really want to help.

Another way I meditate with compassion is remembering the feeding of my infant son. I was lucky enough to be able to breast-feed him, so a wonderful rush of oxytocin, the love hormone, accompanies the feeling of relieving his hunger. Of course, not everyone has breastfed a child, but many of us, both male and female, have bottle fed a child. This can be pictured affectively also. Or, use any memory that stimulates love and the desire to stop someone's pain.

After a few days of practicing compassionate meditation while visioning your own loved ones, transfer those feelings to a stranger. For me it was easy to transfer my feelings to one of the babies that are in war or famine. I can truly feel their suffering and really want to help. You can choose any stranger to transfer your thoughts and feeling towards. After a week of practice, transfer your feelings to the whole world or universe. I transfer these very powerful feelings of compassion for the babies to relieve the hunger of the world. Use whatever you are comfortable with to open yourself to the perfect love that includes everything. Use your compassionate prayer, meditation, or chanting (many people just say Jesus over and over). In 1 John 4 verse 18, we are told, "There is no fear in love. But perfect love drives out fear". Maybe this is the perfect love that is being spoken about? Perfect or whole love is not exclusionary. 1 John 4:1, we are told, "no one has ever seen God; but if we love one another, God lives in us and his love is made complete in us".

To be a temple ready for Divine Energy, whole and healthy, we need to practice compassion. Practicing compassionate meditation activates parts of the prefrontal cortex and the midbrain, and exercises our minds to increase empathy and happy feelings of well-being. Compassion increases the firing of neurons in these areas. The more we practice, the more neural connections, we develop increasing empathy, well-being, and emotional control, and reducing anxiety, depression and negative self-talk.

Compassion may also increase your lifespan. Studies have revealed that people with chronic stress, such as parenting a chronically ill child, have lower telomerase in their cells. Telomerase activity (which is a peptide or protein) dictates how many times our cells divide or reproduce before they die. The lower the amount of telomerase enzyme, the shorter our lifespan. Stress hormones are highly associated with lowered telomerase. Compassionate meditation and deep prayer lowers stress hormones.

When I was sharing about compassionate meditation with a friend, she told me she felt that meditating on loving a hungry child would make her sad. It would make her feel like she wasn't doing enough to help and that the meditation would just make her feel guilty. I told her that she was doing something. Meditation, like prayer is doing something. It not only lowers our stress but it also helps others. From 1982-1985 in the United States and from 1983-1985 in Canada, two studies on meditation found that if the square root of one percent of the total population ($\sqrt{}$ 1% X population) meditated on compassion, then a significant change in the total population is found. The study counted deaths from vehicle accidents, suicides and homicides as the benchmarks to see if the meditation achieved any significant effects. Researchers were thrilled to find a 48% drop in the accidents, suicides and homicides when the population of mediators was above the square root of one percent of the total. The study was published in the U.S. Social Indicators Research 22 in 1990. It is considered blind and respectable because the people that gathered the data on the deaths were blind to the number of meditators and whether the meditators were practicing. A 48% drop in death just because people meditated on peace? That says that we are definitely doing something when we meditate and there are many other studies. Beginning in 1976 with Drs. Borland and Landrith, meditation has continued to be an affective way to reduce crime, violent deaths, auto accidents, and raise the quality of life.

Can you imagine if enough people consciously remembered peace? Would there be any wars left? What is the square root of one percent of the population of the world? The world population is approximately 6.8 billion? It is about 8300 people meditating on peace, or compassionately feeding the world. Only 8300 people! Can't we get 8300 people to be mindful of love? Philippians 4:8 tells us, "Finally, brethren, whatsoever things are true, whatsoever things are honest, whatsoever things are just, whatsoever things are pure, whatsoever things are lovely, whatsoever things are of good report; if there be any virtue, and if there be any praise, think on these things." I think that it is time to take our instructions seriously and start to think on these things and bring changes to our world. Think on love.

Pray Without Ceasing

We are told in 1 Thessalonians 5 verse 17, in Luke 21 verse 36 and in Roman 12 verse 12 to pray constantly. But, does the Bible mean that we should constantly be on our knees asking God for things or saying how great he is? What does praying without stopping mean? According to the Bible, there are three ways to communicate with God: prayer, petition, and praise. Prayer means having open communication, in which one listens as well as talks. Petition is where one lists the things that need to be attended to. Praise means to communicate by glorifying the status of the Divine.

Do we really think God needs our praise? An infinite source of energy, that is all knowing probably doesn't need to be told anything. Praising may be for our health. When we praise and show gratitude, our happiness neuropeptides go up to raise our moods and calm our nervous system. We praise because the Bible directed us to do it. We praise because it uplifts us. It feels good. When we lift our hands up high in praise, the posture itself can change our moods to more positive emotions. Because certain body postures change our moods, even smiling can get us a more positive outlook.

Petitioning or listing our needs and wants is only necessary once. We already know that all things work together for those that love the Lord. So even if it looks like your life is falling apart, and it may well be crumbling, the ultimate outcome will take you to the place that you need to be, emotionally, spiritually, even if it means that physically you are declining. We are all going to give our temples back to the dust and our Spirit energy will return to the one infinite energy field, the place from which all life springs. We are told to never look back to the past and not to bother to worry about the future. In

Luke 9, verse 60, Jesus said, "let the dead bury the dead". We are also told to **ask as if it is already done**. In Mark 11 verse 24, Jesus told us, "Whatever you ask in prayer, believe that you have received it, and it will be yours." Ask as if it is already in the present, in the now, not in the future. We are told to give no mind to the future. We aren't even required to ask for what we need. We are told in Luke 12, verse 27 that the lilies are taken care of and so are we. So we know that praise and petition are not the kinds of prayer that the Bible was talking about when it said to "pray without ceasing".

Prayer, or an open communication line between God and us is already in place. We are told to "be still and know that I Am God". I tried just sitting still, but that didn't really help me to open the communication lines between God and I. My thoughts always took over. My body was still but my mind was busier than ever. So in order to be still completely, I needed to still my mind. The problem grew because the harder I tried to stop my mind, the busier my thoughts became. If I stopped my head for a second, my mind would burst in and congratulate me. If I managed to stop my mind once, I tried even harder the next time. Trying is not the way to stop your mind. Your mind will tell you to try this or try that and the noisy thoughts will get louder the harder you try.

Then, I remembered that we are told by Jesus in Luke 17, verse 21, "The kingdom of God is within you." God is already there. The infinite energy source is already plugged into each and every one of us, listening and talking to us. All we need to do is to start to listen. When I started to listen to what I had always considered emptiness, my mind began to give me space between my thoughts. I began to listen to the empty space between my thoughts. I listened to the empty space between breathes, between musical notes, between the words that people spoke. Quietness began in my head. Sometime I can feel the peace that passes all understanding but it only happens when I stop trying to use my mind to communicate and just listen. Remember, 1 Chronicles 28 verse 9 told us, "if you seek him, he will be found".

Listening to God can be done all of the time if you want. **Quieting your mind by listening to the emptiness that contains the Divine is praying without ceasing.** This is sensible when one remembers that empty space is really crowded with an all-encompassing, all knowing Divine energy source. When I learned to become aware of the space between words, thoughts, emotions, and all other things that want to occupy my mind, I became aware of Spirit there with me. I learned to be still and know God. If you can learn to do this constantly, you can pray without ceasing.

Funny thing is, if I keep a conscious awareness of the emptiness in my head, my emotions and thoughts don't seem so life threatening. Emotions are just floating feelings that I am not connected to. Thoughts are just one possible way of thinking about specific things. Giving Divine consciousness the space to help me gives me a break from being wrapped up in my own needs and wants. Quiet meditation, deep prayer and chanting all decrease stress. They rewire our brains to lower fear and increase well-being.

Dr. Herbert Benson of Harvard Medical School tells us that meditation can come in many forms but it will get you in touch with your body to reduce stress and tension. By meditating, you will begin to walk around more relaxed and be better able to relax when you get stressed. Your concentration and focus will also improve.

Dr. Benson instructs us to meditate by:

- Sitting or lying down
- Repeating a word or just watching our breath

- If the mind wanders gently bring it back to the word or breath
- Practicing 20 minutes everyday

But no matter how you do it, practicing meditation increases a feeling of control, and reduces the number of times we perceive threats or hostility. The more we "be still and know", the more we cultivate emotional balance and awareness of the present. A study published in 2012 by Conscious Cognition, found that long-term mediators change the express of significant numbers of genes throughout their DNA. This means that meditation changes the epigenetic controls over how our bodies make the things we need to stay healthy.

Meditation has been practiced for thousands of years to deepen the understanding of the sacred. Today it is used as a tool for stress reduction. The Mayo Clinic tells us that continuous meditation enhances physical and emotional well-being by eliminating the thousands of tangled thoughts that crowd our minds. It clears your mind to open a space in order to gain new perspectives, increase self-awareness, and build coping skills to manage stress. Meditation creates a state of peace.

Research published by the National Institutes of Health reports that meditation reduces cholesterol, and the chances of heart attack and stroke by 50%. Meditation reduces anxiety, depression and blood pressure. It can turn hopelessness to hope. Paul, in Romans 15 verse 13, wrote "May the God of hope fill you with all joy and peace as you trust so that you may overflow with hope by the power of the Holy Spirit". Being still and knowing God is the way to plug into that power.

How can we concentrate on stillness and continue to go about day-to-day life? Have you ever thought about how many of your thoughts are new? Or, how many of your thoughts are really necessary to your life? We all have thought after thought that is just reliving our past or projecting into our future. Not one of those thoughts ever changed the past or made tomorrow today. The past is always the past and tomorrow never comes, right? The real, necessary thoughts are few and far between, and allow plenty of time between them to continually listen to the Holy Spirit. We just need to be still and know God, know the God that is within us. We can still carry on with our lives. Our lives will become easier, more peaceful. Thoughts suck up our awareness of the Divine. Isaiah, in chapter 32 verse 17, told us, "The fruit of righteousness will be peace; the effect of righteousness will be quietness and confidence forever". We can begin to stop being so reactive. Quietness gives Spirit a chance to take care of things for us instead of our typical jumping to conclusions or reacting out of fear. The Bible tells us to "Seek ye first the kingdom of God and all these things shall be added unto you." Our lives will become better. The petty thoughts will stop getting our attention and give us time to really listen and have peace.

Attachment to anything but the kingdom of God, the now, the present moment, the True-Life form, is just suffering. 1 John 2, verse 15 told us, " Do not love the world. If anyone loves the world or the things in the world, love of the father is not in them". Awareness of the emptiness that contains all power and knowledge is the only way to truly know who you are. Connection with now, the presence of God connects us with this moment, the only thing that there really is. Watching thoughts and emotions as they go by, realizing that they are meaningless puffs of smoke that cannot affect us unless we let go of the awareness of the One. Seek the presence of God within and without and all will be added to you. You can "pray without ceasing", and have an open exchange of communication with the Holy Spirit. This exchange is prayer, not petition, not praise but true listening. When you truly seek God, the one that lives within you, you go to the stillness within. You can open up to the "still small voice". This is how you will know the will of the Divine. We can only seek the Kingdom of God in our own temples. God's home is in you and you can find the Spirit there anytime you want. We are not our histories or our future potential, we are Temples of the Holy Spirit.

The Lord's Prayer

The effects of intercessory prayer, or praying for others, in lab situations show mixed results. One of the hypothesized reasons for these findings is performance anxiety from the patients and angst due to a lack of belief. Anxiety causes more stress, which further decreases health. James wrote in chapter 5 verse 15, "the prayer of faith will save the one who is sick'. One reason faith is required may be to alleviate the anxiety that propagates when someone is aware that they are being prayed for. One study published in 2000 found that remote intercessory prayer decreased duration of fever due to infection, the duration of hospital stay, and the number of deaths due to infections. But, prayer for others, not only helps them, it also helps the people doing the praying. Direct person-to-person prayer lowers cortisol levels and significantly improves depression and anxiety in both people. And, the results can last up to a month.

There are many kinds of prayer. Prayer can change our state of mind instantly. It calms us and brings us to the present moment where all of our bodies systems are working. Mentally preparing to eat is not a new concept. Solomon, the wise king, cautioned us in Proverbs 17 verse 1, "Better a dry crust with peace and quiet than a house full of feasting, with strife". Why better a dry crust? Because eating in a room of anger and disapproval, floods the body with stress hormones, stopping digestion, elimination, and immunity. When this happens we are more prone to the accumulation of toxins and incompletely digested food particles. This can lead to inflammation, allergies and chronic disorders. So how do we prepare ourselves to best utilize the food we are eating?

Being mindful of what and how we eat reminds us to slow down and use all of our senses to engage the act of eating. This lowers stress levels, turns on the parasympathetic nervous system to send saliva and other digestive enzymes to aid our digestion. Mindfulness became a familiar word when Jon Kabat-Zinn, a professor emeritus from Massachusetts Medical School, founded his mindfulness living center in Northern California. The center teaches the reduction of stress, pain and illness through mindfulness and teaches mindful eating. In 2012 the Academy of Nutrition and Dietetics published an article that reported finding that mindful eating significantly lower calorie and sugar intake leading to weight loss and an increase in control over our own health. Why is being mindful of what you eat so important? According to Harvard School of Medicine's Nutrition Department, 75 % of U.S. adults report experiencing stress, 60% report physical symptoms due to stress and approximately 40% increase food intake due to stress. We are bombarded with hectic timetables and pro-eating media that push toxic edible products. It is no wonder that many succumb to fast food.

Mindfulness is the practice of being fully present in each moment. It requires open acceptance of things, as they exist. Mindfulness opens awareness of our feelings, our bodies, our cravings, and our emotions. Practicing mindfulness enhances the awareness of our inter connectedness to others, our communities, our environment, and our universe. It helps us to understand our own beliefs and how they affect us. We must stop living on automatic.

Though the Mindfulness Center teaches from a more eastern philosophy, many of the same instructions can be found in very familiar places in the Bible. In the Lord's Prayer, Christ instructs us to humble ourselves and remember to be in love with and in awe of God, our parent; saying "Our Father in heaven, holy is your name". When we say, "wow, you are great" and feel awe, we are in the present moment or what scientists call being in the flow. Studies published in 2012 by Psychology Science, reported that a sense of awe adjusted participants' sense of time, making them feel less hurried. This helped bring them to the present moment in a calm, patient and satisfied state. Feelings of trust, love and awe or extreme admiration can inspire calmness in the body and mind. We forget our problems, our stresses, and ourselves, and see, taste, touch and smell what is in front of us at that very moment. Becoming aware of the present moment will stop the feelings of never tasting what we eat and wondering why we still feel hungry. So the first part of getting ready to eat is a call to pay attention, to forget ourselves and remember the Divine with a sense of awe.

The second part of the instructions in the Lord's Prayer, "thy kingdom come, thy will be done", tells us to let go of control. If we say to someone, "whatever you decide or want is what I want to happen", then you have let go of control. The second part of the prayer is telling us to give the proverbial steering wheel to the Divine to go wherever. When you let someone else decide how and where to drive, you can kick back and enjoy the trip. Letting go of control is about enjoying the moment, the food, and the company or environment. Literally, we are to say, "whatever you want, my loving, awesome parent". The emotions of respect and love need to be strong enough to bring about the sense of awe that is needed to bring in the present moment. If you are thinking about your business or something else that you need to do later, you haven't followed the instructions.

Asking with the faith of a child is the third instruction. Asking our parent to give us food everyday, as in the words "give us this day our daily bread", requires faith and trust in that parent. Are you still worrying about money and your future while you eat? Christ tells us to put the worry away when we eat. This lowers stress and allows our digestive system to do its work. Pretty simple instructions when you look at it but how many of us pray to quiet our minds before each meal?

Fourth, we are instructed to forgive others and ourselves. We are to put away the past. Any guilt, anger, hatred or resentments need to be released before we eat, every time. This means if we eat three times a day, we put down the heavy bag of the past at least three times. In Proverbs 15:17 King Solomon tells us, "Better a dinner of vegetables where love is, than a steak with hatred". Negative emotions stop our ability to receive the nutrients in the food and cripple our ability to fight any pathogens or toxins that enter the body through our food. Let go of them before you eat.

How we eat makes as much of an impact on our health as what we eat. These steps ensure that we take the time to smell the food. Smelling food starts the enzymes necessary to digest our meal. When we are relaxed, our saliva flows, and our blood, bile, and other digestive enzymes are ready to do their job of breaking down, and purifying what we place in our mouths.

Last, part of the instructions that Christ gave us is really incredible because it showed us that Christ really understood the cravings we experience! The last phrase is, keep us from temptations, cravings, and things that aren't good for us. Wow, I feel so understood! Help me to eat, drink, and do the things that are good for me. Remember, food addiction looks the same on a brain-imaging scan as any other addiction including alcohol, drugs, sex, and gambling. This reference to temptations or addictions was written 2000 plus years ago, before we could scan or test our brains' reactions.

These steps help the meal to satisfy our hungers, quieting our senses by employing them, and giving our bodies the best chance of using the phytochemical nutrients that we need.

When we are present at our meals, we smell, taste, feel the texture, and see the color, freshness, and presentation of the food. We feed our senses and crave less. We become aware of what we are putting in our mouths. This gives us more strength to stay away from things that we would be better off not doing.

Clearing our heads, forgetting the past, and eating in a peaceful environment is the key to digestive health and receiving the maximum nutrients from our food and over time. If practiced each meal, the prayer formula will help to bring your intestinal flora back to health. A healthy microbial community distribution in our Guts will enhance our psychological well-being, hormone balance, immune responses, and the ability to detoxify our systems. It's no wonder that this was Christ's instruction to us before we eat.

This may seem like a lot to do before each meal but it can be condensed to a simple formula, Create awe. Remember the power of the Divine and become aware of where you are. In other words, fill your senses with the wonder of the Divine and the food. Take a minute to smell it. Look at it. It's ok to use your fingers! Touch it. Be at peace. Relax and give control over to the Divine Energy. Trust. Stop worrying about tomorrow. Forgive yourself and others. Leave the past somewhere other than the table. Ask for freedom from cravings. Picking real food, the food that God told us to eat in Genesis 1 verse 29, in the garden, cultivates our internal microbial garden. Eat the fruits of all the plants and trees that have seed. This diet will ensure the correct environment for our friendly microbes and give us the best moods and physical health. That is it, the formula for our healthy eating!

- Come in a state of awe and a quiet mind.
- Relax and enjoy the present moment by giving over control.

- Trust like an innocent child that our needs are given to us every day.
- Forget and forgive any past negative emotions.
- Ask for freedom from addictions.

The directions are so important to the health of our Guts that if you are able to follow them, you can eat things that others, with less ability to relax and trust, can't eat. Paul, in Romans 14:2 told us, "One man's faith allows him to eat everything, but another man, whose faith is weak, eats only vegetables". Weak faith and less trust can cause more stress on our body's systems. We know that additional stress weakens our digestion and immunity. Eating fresh vegetables with all of their phytonutrients and antioxidants might give a highly anxious person the extra nutrients to maintain health, while a person with more trust and less stress may be able to eat anything and still gain nutrients from it. Stress influences our food choices by increasing ghrelin, the hormone that causes us to crave sweet, fatty foods. Stress decreases leptin, the hormone that tells our brain that we have had enough to eat. Using the Lord's Prayer as the guide to preparing to eat is incredibly vital to the health of our bodies' systems.

Do This in Remembrance

I Corinthians chapter 8, verse 8, Paul told us that we cannot win God's approval by what we eat and don't eat. How you eat is as important as what you eat. Having said that, where is the proof? We know that stress redirects our body systems to enable us to run faster and jump higher, in order to run away or win the fight. The fight or flight mechanism floods the brain and the muscles of the legs with oxygenated blood and energy. This shuts down our other systems. If we are stressed too often the shutting down of our digestive and immune systems may have lasting effects. The levels of our digestive acid and enzymes become chronically low and our immune responses are decreased. Low digestive enzymes weaken our ability to digest food and absorb nutrients. A weak digestive system allows undigested food to escape into the blood stream. The escaped undigested food joins protein flags from our immune system called immune complexes, and it ultimately bogs down our whole body.

When we are under stress, our liver is busy making glucose available and not detoxifying the body, especially if we eat late night. Overloaded livers filled with toxins and escaped immune complexes. Undigested foods are the basis of many autoimmune disorders like asthma, eczema, rheumatoid issues, headaches, pain and inflammation. Chronic overload and inflammation allow cancer and virtually all of the leading causes of death, besides accidents, to occur.

Besides learning to relax before we eat, there are other things we can do to enhance how we eat and digest our food. More times than I care to count, I have gulped down the food that was sitting in front of me without remembering eating it. I could swear that someone else ate it when I wasn't looking. I know that this couldn't be true because I was the only one in the room, but it sure felt like it. Eating like that is not satisfying. I didn't taste it. I didn't smell it. I didn't chew it. No wonder I still feel hungry. We shovel our meals down in a rush during a lunch break, or between work and another commitment. We don't pay attention to our bodies' signals telling us what we need to eat and how much. We shovel it in so quickly that we don't give signaling hormones, like leptin, enough time to get the message of satisfaction to our brains. Then, we push away from the table feeling like the over-stuffed chair that we want to go collapse into. Even worse, we eat while driving, stopping at fast food restaurants, eating things that we would never put in our mouths otherwise. You can't argue whether or not you were paying attention to the food while driving, if you were, you are a danger to the rest of the people on the road. We don't have a clue what we eat or how much we eat. It is no wonder that we walk around always craving things, and never quite feeling satisfied. Gulping our food is the first bad habit that must go if we are to receive optimal nutrition from our food.

Taking a moment to be grateful for our food slows us down as well as lifts our spirit. Christ said at the last supper, to take up our cups and remember him. Looking at this from today's point of view, we would be raising our glasses in a toast to remember him. This is not to disrespect the act of the Eucharist, but rather to bring it closer to home, where we can relate to it, and use it to prepare ourselves to get the best nutrition possible from our food.

Remembering the body of Christ when we break bread or raise our cup helps us to understand the importance of remembering the sacredness of food. It helps us to remember that everything is part of the Divine Energy Field. Paul, in 1 Corinthians 10 verse 17 told us, "there is but one loaf and we, who are many, are one body, for we all share the one loaf." Plants and animals, including humans, are all a part of God's universal exchange of energy. When we slow down and become aware of the energy that flows through our food to our body, it reminds us to be at peace and pay attention to the moment. Relaxing ensures the proper levels of stomach acids and digestive enzymes. Remembering the infinite Source, when we break bread or raise our glass, is the perfect recipe for the correct state of mind to eat and derive the most benefit from our food.

How we eat, how much we eat, and what we eat is important to not only the daily maintenance of our body temple but is also important in correcting any past mistakes that may otherwise carry dire consequences. Proper nutrients can even correct epigenetic coding that is passed from mother to child. A prolonged lack of the correct nutrients or a lack during key time frames in pregnancy or infancy can lead to the silencing or activating of genes. But thankfully, there are plenty of paths to correct many of these epigenetic mistakes.

Inflammation is linked to the leading causes of death, such as cardiovascular disease, cancer and type-2 diabetes. These diseases are responsible for almost 70% of the deaths in the United States. Excess fat cells cause inflammation! The more over-weight a person becomes, the higher their chance of inflammation. Modifying our diet and our stress levels can decrease inflammation. Reduced calorie intake and increased phytonutrients from plants can reduce inflammation beyond the reduction of fat cells. Fat cells are hormone producers that cause inflammation and pain on their own. Simply reducing fat cells can reduce pain, heat and inflammation. Losing excess weight decreases the chance of cancer and diabetes. Phytonutrients, or plant nutrients increase our antioxidants levels to decrease free radical damage. They reactivate our DNA transcription to produce factors that protect our bodies from cancer, pain and inflammation. Emotions, behavior and diet work synergistically to magnify the health benefit seen from each one separately, many times over, impacting our absorption, digestion and elimination, allergies and auto-immune disorders, pain levels and even our emotional well-being

Fasting

When we eat is important. Many studies have shown if we practice short fasts on a regular basis, we can also receive great benefits. Intermittent fasts substantially decrease inflammation. Regular periodic fasting balances hormones such as leptin, insulin, and dopamine, and aids in the reduction of weight, lipid counts and blood pressure.

In Isaiah 58 verse 6, the Bible told us that a fast is the way to free ourselves from addictions. "Is not this the fast that I have chose? To loose the bands, to undo the heavy burdens, and to let the oppressed go free, and that ye break every yoke?" These words tell us that fasting can break every addiction. With the scans and other tests available today, research has uncovered why fasts can free us from cravings, disease, and depression. Scans have found links between cravings, obesity, and depression, and have validated that fasts can, in fact, aid the bodies' recovery from these and other issues.

Apart from the obvious drop in calorie intake during a fast, why does fasting help free you from addiction and unhappiness? The answers can now be seen with brain scans. Brain imaging has shown lower dopamine-receptor levels in obese individuals, as well as in the brains of alcoholic and addicts. Hum? Could obesity really be a form of addiction, the same as drugs or alcohol? Studies tell us that alcoholics, drug addicts and obese people all have lower brain dopamine levels.

Dopamine is part of a pleasure feedback loop that creates cravings for foods, drugs, and alcohol. Dopamine, a neurotransmitter or hormone-like messenger, causes a reaction in the brain's pleasure center, the nucleus accumbens. This pleasure reaction sets up a learned reaction, when one sees, smells, or even thinks of the wanted item, dopamine floods the dorsal striatum, the part of the brain that is concerned with experiencing desire or motivation. This sets up pleasure-seeking behavior, a craving for the foods or drugs that we are conditioned to crave. A marshmallow at a campfire, a hotdog at a ballgame, popcorn at a movie, some fast-food during a TV commercial, buying from the ice cream truck on a hot day, or a chocolate bar as a reward for a job well done. We are all conditioned to crave something. Today's media exploits this reward- craving feedback loop. If your dopamine-receptors numbers are lowered from too much of a good thing, your ability to derive pleasure or satisfaction from your food or whatever you are craving is decreased. You then need more to compensate for the loss of activation in your brain's reward circuits.

How is the number of our dopamine receptors decreased? Well, it is just like the down-regulation of insulin receptors. This is how down-regulation happens in regards to insulin. The process of down-regulation occurs when there are sustained, elevated levels of a hormone in the blood. This hormone could be insulin, dopamine, leptin, or many others. The hormone binds to its receptors on the surface of a cell. The receptor helps the hormone to enter the cell. When it enters the cell, the whole hormone receptor complex undergoes endocytosis. Endocytosis is when the cell's membrane forms around the complex or substance, engulfs it, and swallows it. And, just like when food is swallowed, the enzymes inside the cell attack the complex. So not only are the hormone receptors drawn inside the cell with the hormone, they are also actively digested and degraded. In this way, our cells regulate the amount of hormone brought in by the number of receptors they maintain. When the hormone levels are high, increased hormone-receptor binding accelerates the rate of engulfing and degradation. If high levels of binding are sustained, gradually the number of receptors on the cell walls decreases. The more hormone, the faster the receptors are swallowed. This reduces the number of receptors available to bind with the hormones and lowers the signal that is being sent.

Unfortunately, if we keep bombarding our cells with high levels of hormones, the rate of receptor synthesis and insertion into our cellular membranes cannot keep up with their destruction. Although, new receptors are always being synthesized, they are degraded more quickly than can be replenished if the hormone levels remain high. This self-induced loss of cell hormone receptors reduces the cell's sensitivity to the elevated hormone concentration. This affects, not only how our cells are fed, but our moods, weight gain or loss, sleep, and many other things. The process of decreasing the number of receptor sites or down-regulation is virtually the same for all hormones.

Down-regulation of insulin, dopamine or leptin receptors causes the body to become hormone resistant. Insulin resistant cells don't maintain enough receptors to efficiently escort glucose from the bloodstream into the cells or the liver, muscle, brain, adipose or other tissues. This leaves too much glucose in the blood stream. The body responds by further increasing insulin, resulting in a vicious cycle of hyperinsulinemia (too much insulin production), burnout of the pancreas, and type-2 diabetes.

Dopamine resistance is linked to addictive behaviors, cravings and depression. When the dopamine receptors are absent, we indulge in more and more of the things that we crave without feeling satisfied. This is why addicts must continue to use more and more of a substance to feel 'the high' they crave.

Leptin resistance, which is common in over-weight people, reduces the brains ability to tell when we have eaten enough so we eat more to feel full. Leptin also tells the pancreas to stop producing insulin. Sadly, a lack of leptin receptors inhibits the pancreas' ability to hear the signal to stop. So, excess weight and over-eating contributes to continued high levels of insulin, leading to hyperinsulinemia and type-2 diabetes. Add chronic adrenaline, caused by sustained increased stress, and now our bodies don't know when to burn our fat cells for fuel. This causes an inability to reduce weight even if we eat less! Whether high levels of sugar, fatty foods, drugs, alcohol or stress caused the resistance, growing new receptors takes time and requires sustained periods with low levels of the target hormone. This is why we must go 'cold turkey' when we want to stop cravings and addictions. We must give our bodies a chance to play catch up and rebuild our receptors.

Fasting gives our bodies a chance to rebuild the numbers of receptors, but there are many reasons for a fast besides resetting the effectiveness of our hormone receptors. The Bible tells us that fasting can set us free from our addictions, it also tells us to fast when we pray for very important things, or to prepare or discipline ourselves for service as in the cases of Christ, John the Baptist, and Moses and his followers. In fact, in the book of Daniel, fasting was shown to enhance beauty, strength and health. We can use fasting to enhance our immune systems and reduce inflammation; bringing health and beauty back to our body temples.

There are many types of fasts, short or long, very strict or merely limiting the items that we eat. Intermittent fasts can be taken by almost everyone that is in good health. Partial fast like those used for lent, Passover, and fish on Fridays, have been used as a way of disciplining our minds and bodies. John the Baptist partook in this kind of fast with the honey and locust, and manna restricted the diet of the Israelis. Daniel and the other slaves chose a less restricted fast of just fruits, vegetables, and water to prove they didn't need the sacrificed meats and wine.

Long durations of intermittent fasts bring beauty and health. Complete fasts or water fasts surrender our control over ourselves, quickly resetting our minds and our bodies. Jesus used a total or complete fast. Total fasts do their work more quickly, but sometime this is good for the body and sometimes it isn't, depending on how toxic our system is and how strong we are. Knowing which kind of fast is right for you and for how long is a decision for you and your health provider.

Fasting interrupts our hormone feedback cycles. As we have seen by the millions of cases of type-2 diabetes, overwhelming the body with the simple sugars in processed foods can cause a rise in insulin and a subsequent decrease in insulin receptors. This causes our cells to be unable to escort glucose into the cell for fuel. Without insulin as its escort, glucose cannot permeate the cell walls to enter and feed our cells. Our cells start to starve. The high glucose levels in our blood tell our pancreas to make more insulin, causing Hyperinsulinemia and an over worked pancreas. This over working could lead to its shut down. Fasting lowers our blood sugar levels and allows our bodies to slowly increase the number of our insulin receptors.

Of course, this is not the only example of how fasting resets our hormone and receptor levels. Other hormone feedback cycles that are affected by fasting include leptin, ghrelin, serotonin, and dopamine, to name a few. These cycles affect weight gain, cravings, and mood disorders including depression and addiction. Fasting is like cutting off the power supply long enough to reboot the system. Just like an addict's or alcoholic's necessity to completely stop the drug or drink, in order to kick the habit cold turkey; use of a complete or partial fast stops food intake. This gives our cells a chance to build up the number of receptors to allow our neurotransmitters and hormones to function properly. Increasing the number of receptors to normal levels reduces our cravings, and the amount of food needed to satisfy the cravings.

The discipline of a fast also helps to retrain our minds that sugary or fatty rewards are not coming just because we crave them. In Romans 12 verse 2, Paul told us that we can be transformed by the renewing of our minds (resetting) and Isaiah tells us that a fast can be used to loose the bands of oppression and free us from addiction. Galatians 5, verse 1 said that Christ set us free and that we should stand firm to stay away from the yoke of slavery or addiction. What is your addiction, food, alcohol, chocolate, or coffee? Coffee is mine. Juice fasting is the only way is can stay away from coffee. Fasting can free us from cravings and help us to stand firm away from them.

In 2001, a study by the Department of Energy's Brookhaven National Laboratory used Positron Emission Tomography (PET) brain scans to look at the dopamine level of obese and normal weighted individuals. They found that obese individuals had less dopamine receptors than the normal-weighted subjects. They also found that the number of receptors decreased as the mass of the subject increased. In other words, the more obese you are, the less dopamine receptors your brain has to register pleasure and satisfaction. When you eat more carbohydrates, dopamine levels rise causing more receptors to be engulfed. This can really make you a binger or overeater when you are down, and the heavier you become, the more you need to binge.

In 2002, a rat study showed the effects of a junk food diet. Not only were the receptor numbers reduced but the rats didn't want to revert back to a healthy diet. This sounds so familiar. Remember, your dopamine levels may be high but without the receptors to respond to their signal, it may take much more of what you crave to satisfy your craving. This is why a drug addict needs to increase the amount of a drug to achieve the same feeling of elation. PET scans show the same reduction of dopamine receptors in smokers, cocaine addicts, and alcoholics as in the obese. This indicates that chronic overeating is truly an addiction, but we are given a way to break the cycle.

There is only one pharmaceutical drug-free way to loosen the yoke of the world. It is to stop the substance that raises the hormone for which the receptor is decreased. To quit it cold turkey! Fasting allows the body enough time to rebuild the receptors up to a normal level and it stops the cravings that bind us or make us prisoners to our addictions. The only question is how they knew this so long ago. Don't conform to this world! Renew your minds by stopping the cycle of addiction.

Because dopamine and serotonin are linked to well-being and pleasure, down-regulating the receptors of these neurotransmitters can lead to suicidal thoughts, obesity, and major depression. Most of our serotonin is found in our Guts and only about 20% is found in our brains. Knowing this helps us to understand why serotonin is linked to food cravings and satiation. Serotonin re-uptake inhibitors help less than 50% of depressed individuals. Scientists have found that an increase in pre-synaptictic serotonin can cause a concurrent decrease in post-synaptictic serotonin receptor numbers. This decrease in receptor numbers may worsen the depression and thoughts of suicide! This may be why so many young people commit suicide while taking antidepressants. Regulating our hormone receptors through fasting may help to level our moods while using other things such as prayer, meditation, music, nature and working with our hands to enhance our feelings of well-being.

Sugary foods push the serotonin found in our Guts to our brains to create a pleasure signal, but as we have seen, too much of a good thing lowers the receptors available to receive that signal. If we are constantly eating sugary food, the balance of serotonin is off kilter. Our bodies synthesize serotonin and melatonin from the amino acid, tryptophan. Carbohydrates increase the amount of tryptophan in our blood and the serotonin released. Because serotonin is linked to blood pressure, sleep by melatonin, and the control of our moods, many of us have learned to eat high carbohydrate foods to make ourselves feel better. We see high carbohydrate consumption in individuals that are stressed out, and suffering from premenstrual conditions and insomnia. But the bottom line is that too much of a good thing lowers our ability to receive the signals that give us pleasure and we spend our lives muted. Like the way our ears feel after a concert or a very loud noise, we spend our lives in a constant state of muffled senses. We don't give our bodies a chance to rebuild the phones that receive the signals of pleasure, satisfaction, and well-being. Galatians 5, verse 1 told us to go cold turkey and not give up. "It was for freedom that Christ set us free; therefore keep standing firm and do not be subject again to a yoke of slavery."

Often, we make our worst food choices under stress or when depressed. The midnight raid on the refrigerator exemplifies this, because we are too stressed out to sleep. Or, picture the typical scene of the person that was just dumped in a relationship. See them sitting on the couch, shoveling expensive containers of designer ice cream into their mouths, tearfully watching tear-jerking movies. It is so common that it has become cliché. Just de-stressing will decrease binge-eating behaviors. The Bible tells us that fasting should be done prayerfully in a meditative state and with a cheerful face. Posture, smiling, and cheerful words have been shown to help self-correct depression and enhance healing.

Serotonin is higher in animals in environments perceived as having scarcity. If there is less to eat, more serotonin is sent to the brain to keep the brain active, alert and motivated. This keeps the animal looking for food. Without serotonin, the animal (including us) might get frustrated and sleepy, and give up to die in an environment of lack. Fasting enhances mood and increases serotonin. This is why fasting will often give us more energy, especially if the toxin levels in our systems are low.

Limiting what you eat or drink can be effective in helping to clean and detoxify our bodies. John the Baptist limited his diet to honey and locust readying himself for service, and the Israelites were limited to manna in the desert before being ready to enter the promise land. A study published in Lipids in Health and Disease in 2010, found that eating only the food that Daniel ate improved metabolic and cardiovascular health. Aside from the lessons in discipline, limiting your diet to a low calorie, high nutrient-dense food will improve your health and allow your macrophages time to mop up your system. Macrophages are our immune systems cleaning service. While this type of fast may take longer to achieve all of the benefits, it has been shown to have wonderful anti-inflammatory effects. This is due to your immune system ability to clear out the unwanted wastes and toxins. Without the onslaught of external invaders, and the large amounts of nutrient-depleted products and hard to digest foods, macrophages have the time to do their jobs. Increases in antioxidants and micronutrients that we don't receive from processed high calorie foods, aid in healing and beautifying our bodies.

Fasting in a quiet and peaceful state can enhance our health and beauty. Besides the obvious beauty benefits of weight loss, Daniel showed the pharaoh that fasting on water, fruits and vegetables increased their strength, health and beauty. Today, research has shown that resting our digestive system by fasting enhances our immunity, lowers inflammation and allergic reactions. It clears our skin of blemishes and other problems like eczema. Fasting reduces swelling and edema (the water retention in our intercellular jello), and reduces pain. It gives a special kind of white blood cells, macrophages, what the Greeks called "big eaters", a chance to play catch up. If you habitually over-eat, eat hard to digest, fatty or sugary foods, forget to chew or eat when you are stressed, your macrophages have a lot of remedial work to do to insure the health of your cells.

Not only do macrophages attack and eat invaders, they also clean up by eating worn out cells and other wastes in our bodies. Macrophages attack invaders and then give a protein key, identifying the invader or antigen, to another one of our white blood cells, called T-cells. This key is used to initiate a learned immune response and is why we can gain immunity to certain invaders after we have had a disease or a vaccine. This occurs best when our immune system isn't turned off by stress, so calm and quiet is important when one is fasting, as is the happy realization that you are taking care of yourself.

It is very important to fast and eat in a peaceful prayerful or meditative environment because, as we already know, stress decreases the blood supply to our immune and digestive systems. What good does it do if we fast but then stop our immune system from working by being stressed?

If your immune system is working properly and not overwhelmed or stressed, macrophages also clean up cancerous cells in the early phases of tumor development.

Unfortunately, at a certain point, macrophages enter the tumors. With them inside, the tumors have the ability to shut down the macrophage attacks because our bodies no longer recognize the cancer as an invader. This ensures their survival. It is easier for your immune system to prevent cancer at the beginning than to eliminate it once it has really taken root.

Fasting can slow the division rate of healthy cells. This is very useful if one is on chemotherapy because chemotherapy damages the DNA of dividing cells. Fasting protects our healthy cells by slowing cell division. Tumor cells continue very high rates of division during fasting so they are more vulnerable to the chemo than the healthy cells during a fast. In a study of mice injected with a neuroblastoma, a cancerous tumor, scientists found that by starving the mice for 48-60 hours prior to receiving high doses of chemotherapy, all the mice survived with no visible signs of toxicity. Unfortunately, of the mice that didn't fast, over 40% died. We need to remember that our bodies are constantly fighting to keep free of cells that divide incorrectly or become cancerous for one reason or another. We get into trouble when we stop cleaning them up. Fasting helps in the cleaning process.

When we slow the invaders and toxins that enter through our mouths, we give our livers a chance to process our nutrients better as well as remove toxins. This is important because our bodies are open on the inside as well as the outside. We are a kind of bagel or a roll of paper towels. Skin protects our outer layer. If we get a scrap or a small cut, our skin can mend itself. Skin cells constantly lose their outer layer and grow new inner layers just like rolling off the outer layers of the paper towels. Our skin is always sloughing off cells in an almost endless supply of paper towels to use.

The cells of our stomach and intestines do the same thing as our skin cells. Our digestive system interacts and protects us from the outside environment, including microorganisms and pollution. Our skin and gastrointestinal tract both absorb and excrete things. Our digestive system is open to the outside just like our skin. It regulates what gets into the cells and what doesn't. We are open at the mouth and the rectum, and everything in between is a tube that is used to divide what we want inside from what we don't want. Our digestive tract cells, like our skin cells, are constantly sloughing off and making new cells to protect us from acids and digestive enzymes to absorb nutrients.

When we introduce food and drink into the inner tube, we are letting in all kinds of possible invaders. If our tract is in perfect working order, our stomach acids, enzymes, macrophages, and mucus membranes protect us. When we overload our digestive tract, our stomach and intestines have a tough time keeping up with the task. If you add stress and an overabundance of toxins to the already enormous task, you can end up with a weak digestive system. Weak amounts of enzymes may not kill external toxins and may not break down your food properly. This places a strain on the digestion further down the system resulting in undigested particles either reaching the large intestine or the blood stream. These particles can cause huge problems. Some can clog up our lymph. Some, together with lowered digestive enzymes, cause an over growth of the microbes found in our large intestine (dysbiosis), and some escape into the blood stream and form complexes that bind to our tissues

We are used to seeing breaks in the defenses of our skin. When we get a cut or an abrasion, we see redness and swelling around the injury. This is inflammation. It is our body flooding the area with oxygen, nutrients and white blood cells to repair and protect the breach and to fight the invaders that have broken through the stronghold know as our skin. If the area stays inflamed for too long, dead cells and the waste products of the white blood cell and the invaders build up, and oxygen and nutrient levels decrease. This can lead to the death of the cells around the injury. If this dumpsite isn't cleaned up, and the swelling isn't controlled, we end up with chronic problems, permanent damage, loss of tissue, or death. Thankfully, our skin together with our immune system, usually easily overcome the outside invaders and closes up the breach in our defenses.

When our gastrointestinal tract has an injury, it also becomes inflamed and lowers its defenses, though, we may not become aware immediately. Chronic stress decreases blood supply to our digestive and immune systems thus lowering our shields and inviting both an overgrowth of friendly microorganisms that live symbiotically inside our tract, and invading organisms that are not friendly. When this occurs, our body sends oxygen, nutrients, and an immune response to battle the invaders and mend the defenses. But, if stress decreases the response, or inflammation becomes chronic, the invaders enter our cells uninvited. Inflammation can occur not only in response to an injury but also to parasites such as giardia, an overgrowth of candida, or other bacteria like heliobacter, the organism that can lead to ulcers.

Our digestive and immune systems use many chemical weapons to protect us from the outside environment. Some of these weapons cause free radical damage to the healthy cell surrounding the invaders and problem cells. It is very important that these free radicals and wastes are neutralized and discarded. Antioxidants and fiber from plants assist in cleaning up these problems. Antioxidants combine with the ions or free radicals to take away or add the electrons necessary to calm the ions down or render them non-reactive.

Certain foods are very resistant to digestion. They are usually hardy proteins that do not breakdown easily even in stomach acids and digestive enzymes. Imagine how much harder our stomach and intestine need to work, if we gulp down our food without chewing, or if stress decreases our digestion! These proteins are commonly related to food allergies. Some of the most common allergenic foods are dairy, gluten containing grains such as wheat, rye and barley, legumes such as soy and peanuts, nightshades like tomatoes, potatoes and eggplant, many nuts, and corn. These proteins can escape our digestive defenses and get into our bloodstream. They then bind to the sugars in our cell walls changing the cell wall permeability, and causing clumping and unwanted cell division. These changes can cause diarrhea, constipation, sleep disorders, mood swings, memory impairments, sinus problems, and allergic reactions just to name a few.

These binding proteins are called lectins. Though some lectins can help our immunity, these lectins can damage the lining in our tract and can increase the permeability of our membranes allowing unwanted things to pass into our blood system. They bind to the membranes of our intestinal tract and are not broken down. When this happens, our macrophages, which are fairly large, swim in and out between our intestinal cells enlarging the spaces because they sense that something is not correct. This continued enlargement of the spaces between the cells eventually makes it possible for many things to escape into our blood or to other organs. This is known as a leaky Gut. Our bodies try to defend themselves by thickening the mucus that protects itself. A thickened mucus layer can slow down our digestion and lead to imbalances in the microorganisms that grow in our intestine leading to constipation, dysbiosis, and candida or yeast infections.

When a leaky Gut allows these large particles of food to escape from our digestive system, the particles can cause all kinds of havoc. Once they have escaped our natural barriers, these lectins may bind to the surface of cell membranes in arteries, blood vessels, organs, and glands including the thyroid, pancreas, kidneys and adrenals. When this happens, our body sends for our macrophages, more oxygen, nutrients, and other immune responses. This is what we know as inflammation. The area swells, becomes red and painful. Continued inflammation further increases the permeability of our intestinal lining. This allows more toxins into our system, causing a type of feedback loop of continued toxins making the problem bigger and bigger. Our macrophages continue to try to clean up the lectins. Unfortunately, while cleaning up the lectins, which are now bound to our organs and other tissues, our normal cells can be injured and killed by the free radical weapons that our immune system uses to eat up the lectins. This is one of the places we can measure increased photon emissions. When we have reached this point, our macrophages have told our other white blood cells to destroy the lectins. This begins our antibody-antigen or learned key and lock reactions to the escaped food proteins and setting the stage for autoimmune disorders and degenerative diseases. Different lectins are implicated in different diseases. This is just one example of the food we eat making a huge difference in our health. It is not just what food we eat, but how we eat it, when we eat it, and what frame of mind we are in when we eat.

Resting the stomach and intestines allows our immune system to clear out toxins, lectins and other problems such as bacteria and their wastes. Normally, our macrophages remove the lectins that are circulating in our blood, and their wastes or debris are flushed into the lymph, but when we consistently over-eat the wrong foods, eat without chewing, have problems with our digestion or chronically eat under stress, we overload our cleaning system. Once the lectins are bound to the membranes of our tissues, our macrophages sense them as invaders and attack. These attacks are not just on the lectin, but also on the surrounding tissues that they are attached on.

Now our immune system is attacking our body! When our body attacks itself, we call the symptoms an autoimmune disorder or disease. Only this time, we caused it by over-eating and eating the wrong foods. Of course, this is not the only reason we get autoimmune diseases. Lupus is linked to genetic and epigenetic problems with our immune system and others can be linked to bacterial, viral or parasitic infections. Research has shown that resting our digestive system and allowing our immune system a chance to clean up, can decrease inflammation and pain. Fasting allows our immune system to play catch up and concentrate on cleaning up dead waste products and cells that have been taken over by viruses, and cells that contain mistakes in replication that may lead to cancer if not removed.

Fasting can decrease chronic allergies too. When a macrophage eats the escaped lectin it then teaches our T-cells to recognize the protein molecule as an invader. This helps the body to initiate a quick lock and key immune response, the T-cells being the key and the invaders' proteins being the lock. A quick response is important when we are fighting off an invading virus or bacteria, but when the invaders are introduced into our bodies through our Guts and the food we eat, this same response can wreak havoc on our bodies and immune systems. This learned fast immune response initiates the mast cells cascade that we know as an allergic reaction. Cleaning up the lectins, toxins and debris by fasting can help to alleviate sinus, skin, and other problems related to allergic reaction.

Fasting is a way to find out which foods your body has tagged as invaders. After a few days fasting on a simple item such as apples or rice, you can start to add foods back, one at a time. If you add the foods back slowly enough, you will notice if you get a reaction to it. Many people practice the Lenten fast and limit their diets. This kind of limitation is great for your physical health as well as your spiritual one.

Intermittent fasts can also be very effective to restore our health, detoxify and reset our hormone levels, if we practice short fasts on a consistent basis. Short, periodic fasts substantially decrease inflammation and have been show to balance leptin, insulin, and dopamine and aid in the reduction of weight, lipid counts and blood pressure. Research has shown that just altering meal frequency or when you eat can also decrease inflammation levels.

Intermittent fasting is not as difficult as it seems. The word breakfast is descriptive of the short fast most of us take each day from dinner till breaking our fast in the morning with our first meal. For us to derive the greatest benefit from this daily fast, we must stop eating at least three hours before going to sleep and take a short brisk walk or any moderate exercise, lasting 20-30 minutes, after our last meal. This helps to clear the blood sugar from our blood and raise human growth hormone.

Sleep at least eight hours to ensure a long period between our last meal, bedtime and when we eat our first meal. This will greatly increase the efficiency of the liver. An efficient liver regulates our metabolism along with our thyroid. This is one of the reasons why detoxifying and resting our digestive system increases our ability to lose weight and to easily sustain our new weight. It may seem counter-intuitive to rest to lose weight, but when one realizes the timing and interconnectedness of all of our hormones, you realize that everything has equilibrium. While we sleep for a nice long period, our body is packaging all of the nutrients that we gave it into the building blocks and storage units.

Prolonging the period between dinner and breakfast aids in weight loss in another way. When we are fasting, our bodies first use the sugar in our blood, and then the sugar stored in our liver as glycogen. When we have used all of the available sugars, the body goes in search of other storage places to get the glucose that is needed. The hormone, leptin tells the body when to store extra nutrients as white adipose or fat cells. Leptin also tells us when to start using those fat cells for fuel. When we haven't eaten all night, leptin has most likely told our bodies to burn fat for fuel. This throws our bodies into fat burning mode from the moment we awake, so morning is the best time to do a workout. The body will make use of the fat cells because the readily available sugars have already been used as fuel during the night.

These healthy shifts in behavior can make a difference in the levels of our allergies, pain, inflammation, weight loss, blood sugar, and feelings of well-being. If you eat only real foods and not processed food products, the results may astound you and everyone around you. It will aid in balancing hormones, reducing fat cells, blood sugar, and cravings.

Sugar, in the form of glucose, is the energy or fuel for our bodies. When we eat, our bodies immediately start to use the glucose in our bloodstream. If there is an abundance of glucose the liver packages it and shuttles it into our white adipose cells, better known as fat cells for storage. If we give the body a long enough period between eating, we use up all of the glucose in our blood, then we use all of the sugar stored as glycogen. When we have used all the available sugars, the body goes to other storage places to get the glucose that is needed. Our bodies' storage of glucose is found in our fat cells. While we are asleep we start to use our stored energy. So, when we wake up, after a good night's sleep, we are already in fat burn mode. To really utilize this mode, we can extend the time in between eating and we can exercise for about thirty minutes upon rising each morning to burn off more fat cells. This exercise must be done with a completely empty stomach before you put anything, even coffee with cream in your mouth. The calories you burn will take off fat.

This is so important that it bears repeating, fat cells make their own hormones! Leptin is the hormone that tells the body when to store fat. It also tells us when we are full. Our white adipose or fat cells secrete it. That means our fat cells are part of our endocrine system along with our thyroid, pituitary, adrenal and other glands. Leptin signals the brain to influence our appetites, our metabolism and when we burn our fat cells for fuel. When we were hunter-gatherers, we needed to store food for the winter or any other time of lack. The more fat cells you stored the better able you were to survive famine. This ability to conveniently take food with us was very important. Just like hamsters stuffing their cheeks with food to take with them, we stored food as fat, which freed up our hands for carrying or doing other things. Fortunately or unfortunately, we no longer need to survive long times without food.

Leptin also interacts with the functioning of our insulin cycles, growth hormones, sex hormones (affecting fertility), adrenal function, stress hormones, thyroid function and inflammation. Although leptin's major function is to control and coordinate our metabolism and to prevent starvation, scientists have identified at least fifteen other signals coming from fat cells or white adipose tissue. When the leptin levels are normal, the hypothalamus signals fullness and our metabolism goes up. We are able to burn fat cells for fuel and no more are made.

When we chronically over-eat, our leptin receptors become resistant. Our brains become unable to sense when there is enough leptin to stop storing fat and release them for fuel. Our leptin levels in our blood may be high but the brain doesn't receive the message so we still feel hungry and continue to pack away fuel for later as white adipose tissue.

Research has shown that blood leptin levels are high in obese women but decreased in women with low body weight. Leptin resistance is one of the primary reasons for obesity. If we don't know when to stop eating or when to stop stocking up fat for a rainy day, of course, we are going to have more fat cells. But, it gets even more complicated than that; the more fat cells you have the more hormones are made and sent around your body. Additionally, leptin resistance induces insulin resistance and then adrenaline resistance.

As we know, the amygdala signals the hypothalamus when there is a threat. The hypothalamus then sends a message down to the adrenals to release adrenaline. This sympathetic response stimulates the adipose tissue to release energy and raise our metabolism for fast response to survive. This is why, when our leptin levels are normal, we tend to lose weight when under physiological stress. But, when we become leptin resistant from chronic over-eating our brains release adrenaline to stimulate the metabolism. If this compensation is accompanied by chronic stress, the body becomes adrenaline resistant. Excess stress, assertive behavior, or hard physical labor can cause excess adrenaline. If stress is sustained, we become adrenaline resistant. Our metabolism never rises, fat cells continue to be made, and neither, leptin or adrenaline can signal the release of fat cells for energy.

Eating causes sugar to enter our bloodstream. This stimulates insulin production. Insulin then stimulates leptin production. Normally, when leptin levels reach a high enough level, leptin signals for the insulin production to turn off. If our body becomes leptin resistant, then our pancreas never gets the message to stop the production of insulin. The problem with nonstop insulin production is that insulin promotes leptin production and promotes fat accumulation at the same time! So we continue to accumulate fat cells, mostly around our waists, because there is no feedback cycle to shut off the insulin. If we eat processed or highly sugared food, we make this problem even worse. Sustained high levels of insulin lead to insulin resistance, pancreas burn out and type-2 diabetes.

So you can see how chronic over-eating leads to leptin resistance, insulin resistance and adrenaline resistance. This resistance can lead to weight gain especially around the middle, cardiovascular problems including high blood pressure, inflammation, and difficulty sleeping. If we can't get energy from glucose, then we will feel fatigued more easily and often. We sometimes call this chronic fatigue. In Proverbs 23, verse 21, we are warned not to eat or drink too much "for drunkards and gluttons become poor, and drowsiness clothes them in rags". Chronic overeating or over-drinking of high sugar fluids, including alcohol, colas, etc., lead to fatigue or burn out.

I find it interesting that the seven deadly sins or carnal sins (which are not found as a specific list in the Bible), all lead to an increase of one or more of the hormones involved in these feedback cycles. Anger, lust, pride, coveting, and jealousy all raise stress hormone levels. Gluttony raises insulin and leptin, and sloth or laziness keeps us from decreasing the hormones naturally and easy. A little exercise, after each meal and before breakfast, uses blood sugar to decrease insulin and to burn adipose tissue lowering the amount of leptin produced. Exercise also decreases stress hormones.

Leptin levels also affect our moods and our cravings. Research has shown that leptin has a direct influence on the amount of dopamine circulation in our brains. If our brains are leptin deficient due to leptin resistant obesity, we will have stronger cravings and find it harder to resist them. This is also why when you initially start your fast, you may feel very strong cravings and hunger pains. Leptin levels in the brain are strongly linked to our dopamine levels. Dopamine is part of our reward and motivation system. We must reset our leptin levels to undo the damage of leptin resistance. Studies on fasting rats showed significant increases in dopamine levels. Obesity will always prevail if we don't reset our metabolic signals of satiety to regain control of our appetites. Philippians 3, verse 19 again cautioned us, "Their destiny is destruction, their God is their stomach, and their glory is in their shame. Their mind is on earthly things". How can our minds be on Divine things when we are fighting cravings and appetites all of the time?

Excess white adipose tissue can cause inflammation. Yes, just being overweight can cause pain and swelling of joints and other places in our bodies. This pain is over and above just carrying the extra strain that the pounds put on our bones, muscles and other tissues. Chronic inflammation can lead to heart disease, cancer, and arthritis. Ridding our bodies of excess white adipose cells lowers inflammation and autoimmune responses.

Leptin resistance is also linked to alcoholism and drug abuse. If these toxins are chronically found in our system, they will bog down our livers. A sluggish liver means a sluggish metabolism, which makes losing weight even harder. How do we free ourselves from these bonds? Try a fast! Intermittent fast, short fast, long fast, limited food fast, juice fast, a fast with friends, or a total fast, it is up to you, but try it at least once a week if your health allows you. It will give your digestive system a rest and your immune system a chance to clean up, but most of all it will reset the levels of your receptors and reduce your cravings.

In Romans 8 verse 13, we are told; "For if you live according to human nature, you are going to die, but if by the Spirit you continually put to death the activities of the body, you will live". If we continue with the bad habits and addictions of the flesh, we will die sooner than the one hundred and twenty years that are promised to us. None of us want to be taken apart piece by piece like people suffering from neuropathies due to diabetes or to slowly waste away from cancers. Human nature is to crave the things that make us feel good. Unfortunately too much of a good thing is too much of a good thing. The Bible tells us that fasting is a way to curtail these cravings and habits of the flesh. Clearly, again freewill reigns giving us the choice.

To Everything There is a Season

Everything has its timing. Ecclesiastes 3 tells us that there is a time for every activity. What season you were born in and the amount of vitamin D your mother produced may have affected your possibility of contracting diseases such as Muscular Dystrophy. How much light energy we get is very important. Without the sun, we cannot produce the vitamin D necessary for our bodies. Lack of vitamin D is linked to autoimmune disorders as well. How much sun our bodies take in is so important, that it is believed that humans mutated to lighten our skins in the areas of the world that don't receive enough sun and to darken in the places that get too much. This mutation protects us from making too much or too little vitamin D. Sunlight nudged our epigenetics toward protecting our bodies from ultraviolet waves while allowing enough sun to filter in to make vitamin D.

The rise and fall of the sun in the sky regulates our sleep, if artificial lights don't interfere. Rising with the sunlight and going for a short 20 to 30 minute walk first thing in the morning, helps to set our internal clocks by converting our melatonin back into serotonin. Sunlight turns on serotonin and its lack keeps melatonin in our systems. So, along with the morning walks, it is important to sleep at night in a completely dark room. Melatonin helps us to sleep, enhances immunity, and lowers the affects of stress. When it is dark, melatonin is produced in the pineal glands in our brains. The correct cycle between serotonin and melatonin balances our moods, regulates our sleep cycles, and increases our energy levels and feelings of well-being. Light photons or their lack set our internal clocks and influences our hormone levels.

Living very far north in the winter months, can cause seasonal affective disorder (SAD) and increased rheumatoid arthritis symptoms. SAD can manifest as depression or bipolar disorder. Lack of sunlight can be counteracted by light therapy using blue lights and melatonin can be added to your diet. Besides being synthesized in our bodies, Melatonin can be found in foods such as cherries and rice, and herbs like feverfew and St John's wort. Besides inducing drowsiness and nudging the time you can fall asleep, melatonin is a powerful antioxidant. It protects our mitochondria from free radicals. It is anti-inflammatory, and has been used to counteract autoimmune diseases and fight infectious diseases. The timing and amount of sunlight affects more that just our sleep patterns. Photons from the sun protect our health.

Our circadian rhythms or internal clocks control more than just our sleep patterns. Sleeping 8 to 9 hours a night normalizes our hormone cycles including insulin, serotonin, ghrelin, leptin, norepinephrine, and growth, sex and stress hormones. This means that our internal clocks influence our fertility, immunity, stress levels and even our appetites! Sleeping can reset our stress levels and help us to relax. *Early to bed, early to rise, keeps a man healthy, wealthy, and wise* is again not just an empty saying but a scientific fact. Restoration of sleeping cycles helps to restore our endocrine system to balance.

Digestive enzymes, bile, and liver function are also important to restoring health. Night eating is one of the common challenges of stressed-out, obese women. If you get up in the middle of the night to eat, eat a large amount of calories and then skip your morning meal, you are doing more than just adding calories to your diet. Night eating can disrupt the natural rhythms of our hormones including insulin, leptin, norepinephrine, as well as sex-linked hormones and hormones linked to anxiety and depression. It interferes with the liver's work of filtering toxins and packaging nutrients leading to a sluggish metabolism and over-loaded immune system. The timing of your meals can cause gain weight!

Eating a larger morning meal (as a reward for not eating at night), a leafy green and cruciferous vegetable lunch, and a small evening meal followed by a walk help to balance our growth hormones and insulin. A cup of herbal tea that can contain, hops, valerian, lemon balm, passionflower, chamomile, St. John's wort or one of the many other soothing teas can help to induce sleep in a timely fashion. If you wake up to eat, fight the urge and promise yourself a reward in the morning. The reward that I tell myself at night is the promise of a great cup of tea and sprouted grain toast with almond butter and pure fruit spread. Find a reward that works for you. Keep the light off and stay in bed. Not eating at night can help to bring your levels and cycles back to normal. Most adults need to sleep between 7 ½ to 8 ½ hours to allow our livers to process our foods, fats, toxins, and wastes. Not getting enough sleep can throw our bodies' rhythmic clocks off, leading again to a disruption of hormones. But, these disruptions can also happen in reverse. A decrease in the neurotransmitter serotonin leads to a lack of melatonin, which can affect our ability to sleep. So, making sure to get the correct nutrition to maintain serotonin is also important. If the rhythmic clock that directs the rise and fall of hormones is shifted, the cravings to get up and eat in the middle of the night are increased.

The inter-relatedness between photons, hormones and cravings indicates how important the timing of sleep and nutrition is to the health of our temples' systems. Ensuring a long period between our last meal, bedtime, and when we eat our first meal will greatly increase the efficiency of our liver. An efficient liver along with our thyroids regulates our metabolisms. This is one of the reasons why detoxifying and resting our digestive system will increase our ability to lose weight and make it easy to sustain our new weight.

Too many fat cells are linked to chronic inflammation. Inflammation is linked to chronic diseases like cancer and heart disease. Fat cells are an endocrine organ. And yes, they make their own hormones. These fat-made hormones regulate whether we feel hungry or not. Boy, talk about giving the keys of the jail to the prisoners! Similar to insulin resistance, we can become leptin resistant. Leptin resistance damages our ability to gauge when we have eaten enough. How do we fix our hunger gauge? One way is to do short intermittent nightly fasts!

If we can extend the period of fasting between dinner and breakfast to last between 12 to 16 hours per night, we can, with the addition of 30 to 40 minutes of exercise before eating our first meal of the day, really accelerate weight loss, detoxification, and the return of our hormone to their correct circadian rhythm cycles. This is as simple as eating before 6:00 pm the night before, taking a walk before bed, sleeping 8 hours, and waking up to a 30-minute exercise DVD or routine before eating.

When we eat and sleep helps to regulate the rhythms of our hormones, and controls our immunity, our fertility, how fast we age, and our sense of well-being. Prolonged stress causes higher levels of serotonin in our brain and less in our Guts. Increased brain serotonin levels lead to serotonin resistance and the depletion of the protein, tryptophan. Eating your carbohydrates in your evening meal causes a release of tryptophan into the blood, which enables the body to synthesize serotonin, especially if the protein eaten is from a vegetable source. The insulin released to escort the sugars made from the carbohydrates helps to lower the transport of other competitive proteins. This increases the tryptophan available to make serotonin. Serotonin helps us to adapt and cope.

The resetting of our internal clocks balances our hormones and neurotransmitters, improves our moods and immunity, and lowers our cravings and stress. Like winding and setting a clock, the photons from the sun, provide the exact timing and rhythms for ideal health. There is a time for everything, and a season for every activity under heaven.

As a Man Thinks in His Heart, So Is He

Food addictions and cravings have an emotional attachment as well as a physical one. When it comes to food, it is often difficult to throw off the past. Romans 14, verse 17 reminded us, "For the kingdom of God is not a matter of eating and drinking, but of righteousness, peace and joy in the Holy Spirit". If the family table was far from a righteous, peaceful and joyful time, it can be hard to simply sit down and enjoy a meal. The stress level was so high in my house; I became unable to eat normally. My digestion and elimination eventually slowed to almost a complete halt. My metabolism suffered from my intermittent food intake. Conversely, along with past emotional triggers, food can sometimes be used to stuff emotions and fill needs. A man, I know called Tom, is a successful businessman. He is well thought of in his community, at his work and at his church. Always a stocky kid, Tom gained even more weight as he got older, especially around the middle. He battled allergies and began taking medicine daily to alleviate his sinus symptoms. His weight continues to climb and soon his doctor added Statin drugs to lower his high cholesterol to the allergy medications that he was already taking each day. Like 70% of the people with high cholesterol, Tom didn't change his diet, his exercise routine, or his lifestyle.

Soon after, Tom was diagnosed with type 2-diabetes. He was given another prescription for more medicine to take each day. Tom had a terrible time balancing his blood sugar, while he ate the foods he had always eaten. He became depressed by the bad news about his health and began to binge on alcohol. Tom was now up against a wall. If he didn't control his diabetes, he could face blindness, a loss of limbs or even death. But, Tom had formed attachments to certain foods at specific times of the day. He loved his sweets late at night. Tom would stay up very late, go out and drive through a fast-food restaurant to get his fix of sweets.

Now, you could say this makes Tom sound really lame, right? Wrong, I could tell you the same story for many men and women I know. Only about 20 to 30 % of the people diagnosed with metabolic disorders such as type 2-diabetes, high blood pressure, high cholesterol, insulin resistance, and excess weight around the middle, change their lifestyle. The same is true for those with heart disease. Each disease may seem different but the results are the same: chronic illness, perpetual prescription medicine, and doctor's visits that don't cure the disease but only control the physical symptoms. These medications often cause even worse side effects.

The reason I am telling about Tom is this; he is a successful man! A long marriage, a good position, good provider for his family, and respect from social groups; from the exterior you would perceive Tom as in control of his life. Unfortunately, when Tom tried to change his eating habits, he ran into the same challenge over and over. If he was going to change, he believed that someone else had to take responsibility for his eating. To hear him talk, it sounded like he wanted his mother to take responsibility. That is, in fact, what he wanted! Tom was raised by his great aunt without much affection. As we spoke, he conveyed that he still felt the emptiness of loss where his parents should have been in his Gut. Yes, if you think about it, often we feel loss as a yearning in our Guts. Its no wonder we eat to fill it.

The Bible refers to the Gut as our bowels. We can all relate to a churning in our Guts. The Gut is the center of most of the serotonin in our bodies. Maybe today's translation of bowels would be better understood as our Gut. We use the word in our everyday language when we say things like, "Do it from the

Gut". "It takes Guts," a call for courage is one aspect, but "following our Gut instinct" is about our intuition. "I felt like I was hit in the Gut" is the feeling of being stopped in our tracks, and our breath and our motivation being taken away. The Bible refers to the feelings of joy, anguish and compassion when speaking of the Gut or bowels. Whatever the reference, our Guts are the seat of very intense emotions and these emotions have a very strong affect on our whole body.

How do we rein in these emotions, in order to maintain the health of our lives and our health? In 2 Corinthians, the King James translation talked of being restrained by our own Guts. We are limited by our own perceptions and blocked emotions. Tom's past belief patterns and emotions connected to them were still ruling him. This is like letting a five-year-old rule your life. You can use your cortex to alter your beliefs about the past and yourself. Truly changing what you believe changes your emotions, hormones, stress levels and even our cravings. The question is do you actually trust that you are a temple of the universal source? Remember, trust is based on past experiences. With the facts provided by biophysics and other sciences, we no longer must base our lives on faith. We actually do house the infinite energy that makes the universe!

Many times the Bible translates the word 'bowels' as heart and speaks of the refreshing of our Gut through the encouragement of others. When we block emotions, we block compassion. Philemon 1, verse 20, directed us to find encouragement from others to relieve the yearning and churning of our Guts caused by emotions. We need others to encourage us to help relieve the emotions that hold us back from health and happiness.

Why is the health of our Guts so important? Scientists are now calling the Gut our second brain or the enteric nervous system.

This Gut-based nervous system is made up of myelin-sheathed neurons embedded in the walls of our Gut. There are around 100 million neurons in our so-called second brain. It contains more neurons than our spinal cords. Though our enteric brain doesn't think higher thoughts like figuring out a math problem or making decisions, about 90% of the connections from the Gut's primary nerve, the vagus nerve runs up to our brain. These connections send signals or messages about our feelings or emotions. Our Guts send intuitive feelings directly to our brains. The churning or boiling in our Guts sends an emotional message by interpreting the physiological affects of the stress on our digestive system.

Scientist's can apply electrical impulses on the vagus nerve to alleviate depression. Why does this work? Our Guts tells our brains how we are feeling. Over 30 neurotransmitters are found in our Guts and 95% of our serotonin is stored there. Our brains communicate with our Gut microflora, both the beneficial and the pathogenic ones, by releasing and receiving signal molecules to and from the Gut space. These messages come from our neurons, immune cells, and special neuroendocrine cells in the Gut's lining.

These special cells called enterochromaffin cells react to flavors and odors, as well as other signaling molecules to release serotonin and regulate motility and secretions. They also talk to the microbes in our Gut. This discovery of how scents and odors help to regulate our Gut motility and secretions helps to explain why aromatherapy works and why smells can trigger nausea or other problems. Our brain communicates indirectly with our Gut microbes by changing Gut motility, secretions, and permeability.

Enterochromaffin cells are found at the interface between the 10-100 trillion microorganisms inside of our Guts and the branch of the vagus nerve that sends messages to the brain.

These cells are full of serotonin and other signaling molecules. This nerve pathway modulates our sense of well-being and our moods, as well as motility and secretions. These cells tell our intestines to start peristalsis and the removal of toxins. Our Gut microbes appear to affect our anxiety and stress responses. Use of probiotics can be useful in treating some psychological distress. Why would this occur? If our Gut, microbes, and brain systems aren't working well, we can't release toxins and absorb nutrients. This makes us feel terrible. If this state becomes long-term, as in chronic constipation or irritable bowels, it shifts our microbial garden. This alters the signals for serotonin and other molecules causing us to become depressed, anxious and even panicky. It makes us 'feel like crap' or any other word that we use to describe fecal matter. We may be "full of it" or we could become panicky or anxious due to the unpredictability of our system.

Why does this happen? There are many reasons, but basically our intestinal cells pick up signals from our microbes and from our neurons in the walls of the Gut. They relay those messages up through the vagus nerve tract and through the spinal cord to our emotional brains. These messages can affect our digestion, elimination, immunity, and psychological well-being. The enterochromaffin cells release serotonin in response to irritations, toxins, and changes in the pressure in the cell walls. They signal the vagus nerve and the microbes. These signals lead to feeling of depression and the over all feeling like 'pooh', because they affect bowel function too.

All of these malfunctions can lead to inflammation and permeability of the Gut walls. When the Gut begins to leak toxins, undigested food, and unfriendly microbes into the body, allergies, asthma and autoimmune diseases can begin. Other causes of Gut malfunctions include: genetic factors, early life experiences, infections, inflammation, unfriendly Gut microbes, as well as emotional and psychological disturbances. The translation of all of this is that Gut problems are caused by diet, calorie intake, eating patterns, lack of exercise, smoking, alcohol, coffee, sleep patterns and emotional states.

Like many of the body's signaling systems, the serotonin released from the Gut is involved in a feedback loop system. When the Gut-microbe-brain system is disturbed, negative feelings, low serotonin, and elevated stress occurs. Stress is another major factor that disrupts the Gut-microbe-brain system. Other disrupters include infection and antibiotics. These infections often hit during or following a stressful event.

Loss, abuse, neglect and other stresses often alter a child's physiology and the way a child responds to stresses. These changes are sometimes called hyper-vigilance or posttraumatic stress. The child's amygdala responds faster. They never relax or let down their guard. This hyper-responsiveness sends more fear signals and stress hormones around the body slowing digestion, and affecting elimination. This changes the internal fiber garden and microbial zoo that grows inside of the child's Gut. Hyper-vigilance, a constant state of attention on things that produce fear, causes an over use of stress hormones and receptors, and it leads to adrenal burnout and depression, lowered immunity, anxiety and even panic attacks.

Believe it or not, clinical studies have shown that one of the best ways to start the correction of a hyper-vigilant state is to believe in something or to have faith in something bigger than you. Just as Jesus said in Mark 5, verse 34 and Luke 8, verse 48, "your faith has set you free, go in peace", we can be set free of our fear and negative emotions. This freedom literally heals us. We can, "go in peace and be free from suffering". Has Tom changed to protect his health? Not yet, but I hope that he will soon, by altering his beliefs and emotions connected to his past. Truly, we are all like Tom in one way or another, and we all can free ourselves by the renewing of our minds!

Changing our stress is about adjusting our coping skills to include a new belief or thought system, and incorporation of deep prayer, meditation or biofeedback. This should come as no big surprise as we are told to be still and know God, pray without ceasing and become new. New beliefs can truly change the way your DNA is used to keep and return your body to health by shutting down the stress hormones. This allows all of the systems in your body to return to working order, and return the gardens inside of our Guts to a happy balanced fertile place where friendly microbes prevail. Yes, if we stay in the garden, we live happy, healthy lives. Living outside of the garden is a sulfur-smelling hellish environment of sickness and unhappiness.

Altering our beliefs to alleviate fear and addictions is the number one place to start to rebuild our health. This is why changing how you look at the world around you is so important. Continuous catastrophic or worst case thinking is common to people that live in fear or stress. "Becoming a new person, continually renewed in the knowledge to be like your Creator," is the decision to see Divine Energy or Holy Spirit all around us and in us. We are safe because we house the Holy Spirit in our temple. Believing that the Divine Energy, which makes up the universe, is residing in our bodies can free us from fear. Like any parent, our Creator loves us. To become still and know God, gives us a sense of how much love there is. And, 1 John 4, verse 18 told us that 'perfect love casts out fear'. Stopping fear heals our bodies. We are eternal lights in the form of matter and energy cannot be destroyed. We cannot be destroyed. We have nothing to fear. Following the instruction in the Bible enables us to build beliefs that can get us back to the internal garden of health found in our Guts.

Back to the Garden

The clean-up cycles on the Earth are perfectly in balance when humans are left out of the equations. The clean water, soil and air recycled by these systems are vital to our health. Unfortunately, human-made and altered products, such as plastics manufacturing, mining and pesticide use, cause toxins to shift the balances of the Earth's cleaning systems. Plastics, aluminum and other toxins also pollute the internal gardens inside of our Guts. Some plastics pretend to be hormones. They attach to receptors and won't let go. These hormone mimickers and other toxins can cause birth defects and cancers. Plastics and other toxins can also cause long-lasting changes in the microbial communities inside our intestines.

Our Gut communities powerfully influence our physical and emotional health. A polluted internal garden affects everything from our moods and anxiety, to how well we deal with the die-off and clean-up of the cells that cause cancers. Metals like aluminum, cadmium and lead can roam around our bodies pulling off electrons and setting off a tug-of-war-like fight. This war over electrons can cause a cascade of free radicals yanking electrons from wherever they can, and ultimately producing inflammation, pain and disease. These are only a few of the human-made dangers held in the water we drink, the air we breath, and the ground we live on. Toxins destroy our internal gardens. The bottom line is the external environment affects our internal environments.

Many of us don't realize that we have more microbes inside of our Guts than we have cells in our bodies. We have many of the same microbes as the soil garden of the earth, which is home to even more. We come from the dust of the Earth. Ecclesiastes 12, verse 7, told us that, "For then the dust will return to the earth, and the Spirit will return to God who gave it." Spirit energy, the breath of God, spontaneously begins a wave of current through our brains, our nerves and our hearts when we are being made in our mother's womb. The Bible says that this spontaneous energy will return to the Divine. It also reminds us that our physical bodies will return to the physical elements to be recycled by our microorganisms, insects, and plants.

We are intimately interconnected with the Earth's systems. Without the elements found in the atmosphere, water and soil, we could not continue to exist. Elements are the simplest units of all the substances that we know as matter, like carbon, hydrogen, oxygen, etc. Most elements act like little magnets to make and break bonds or relationships with each other to form molecules. They use proton-powered electrons to create and sever their bonds. Two atoms of the element, oxygen creates the molecule we breathe. A molecule of three oxygen atoms produces the ozone that protects us from the ultraviolet waves of the Sun. Carbon molecules form the carbohydrates, fats and proteins that we eat and that we are made up of.

Everything is constantly renewing and we are becoming increasingly aware of the need to recycle these same elements back, in a clean fashion, to keep the systems functioning. The earth continually produces a new crust, pushing up melted magma while pulling down the old crust into the earth's core. High temperatures and pressure gives birth to crystals and glass. Rock bubbles up from the center of our planet and is broken down by mechanical means such as wind, heat, ice or water. Rock is also chemically weathered by things like salt and biologically weathered by lichen (kind of a cross between a fungus and a photosynthetic algae) and mosses.

Lichen grow to form the fuzzy multicolored mosaics on the faces of boulders. Lichen can use nitrogen and water from the atmosphere, the photosynthetic energy of the sun, and the minerals from the rocks to grow. Lichen eat rock. They are one of the first to colonize the rocks. Lichen growth processes and eating, along with other types of weathering, help cause a breaking down of the rock into regolith or baby soil. Plants can then begin to colonize the brand new soil.

Like pulling a rabbit out of a hat, certain microbes pull nitrogen from thin air and package it so plants can easily use it. If we didn't have these fungi, algae, bacteria and other microorganisms to break down the soil and the rotting of dead matter, and to recycle nutrients, we would be swimming in dead tissue and other wastes. Just as importantly, without microbes plants would become malnourished and be unable to produce the food that we and other animals need. In Genesis 1, the Divine said, "Let the land produce vegetation"…"and he saw that it was good". The land and the microbes within it, are critical to the production of the food we eat, and without good soil and healthy microbes, no nourishing food is grown. Chemical fertilizers only provide a few major elements that are used, as nutrients by plants, so they further deplete the soil of other needed nutrients. Scientists simply don't know enough to imitate natural cycles yet.

Plants are like little solar power factories. With the help of microorganisms, water and fertile soil, plants construct carbohydrates, proteins and fats from light energy. Plants are our main supply of nutrients and energy. Even if we eat animals, most of their growth is due to plant nutrients, so we are just getting plant photon energy indirectly. They store the photon energy from the sun in their tissues and we break down that solar fuel to build our proteins, fats and other building blocks. The photons from the sun fuel everything on the earth from photosynthetic microbes and plants, to the animals, including us, that eat them. Photons even power the evaporation that causes rain and the air currents (along with the spin of the Earth) that cause wind.

Plants store most of their photosynthetic energy in the form of carbohydrates. When we break down those carbohydrates, we get energy in form of sugars, fibers, vitamins, minerals and other phytonutrients. We inhale oxygen to burn the energy that come from carbohydrates, and return water and carbon dioxide to the earth. Plants recycle the carbon dioxide that we exhale by breathing it in and exhaling oxygen. Like gasoline engines, which combine hydrocarbon fuel (gas) and oxygen, our cells use the energy from plant carbohydrates and oxygen as our main fuel.

While plants provide us with fuel, fiber and protein building blocks, they also provide many other nutrients. Phytonutrients are the nutrients and other chemicals that come from plants. Though scientists have isolated thousands of phytochemicals and are constantly finding more, they only know a small amount about them. We know them as vitamins, minerals, bioflavonoids, alkaloids, antioxidants, and aromatics to name a few. What we do know is this: when we don't eat a large diversity of plants from fertile soils, we run the risk of not getting enough phytonutrients and becoming malnourished. These deficiencies can alter the way we make our proteins. Chronic deficiencies can lead to premature aging and disease.

Like us, plants use biochemical weapons to survive. Plants fight the same elements we do. Without legs to move from an inhospitable place, plants must adapt to pollution, parasites, insects and other diseases, and lack of nutrients. Plants are master adaptors. They adapt by forming new phytochemicals to stop diseases, parasites and insects. Coffee is a great example of how plants avoided being eaten by insects. Caffeine is a neurotoxin that certain plants produce. It is a nerve weapon of mass destruction. When an insect eats the plant, the caffeine causes a reaction in their nervous systems that shakes them to death. You can understand why coffee can give you the jitters! The chemical toxin protects the plant, enabling it to grow without fear of being completely eaten. Plants' green leaves are their solar factories most of the time, although green stems and bark can be used too. It is imperative that plants have the correct number of leaves or right amount of green surface exposed to the sun to generate fuel for tissue production and reproduction. If there is too little green surface to photosynthesize, the plant is stunted or dies. If there is too much green area exposed to the sun, the plant dries up. Plants have to create phytochemicals to survive. With care, we can use these phytochemicals.

Plants form synergistic relationships with helpful microbes. One example of this kind of sharing is the exchanging of plant carbohydrates for the easily digestible nitrogen made available by the microbe. The microbes eat some of the plant carbohydrates and give the plant nitrogen in return. Peanuts and alfalfa utilize Rhizobia bacteria in this fashion. Making nitrogen available to plants is a matter of changing the number of electrons it has and the form it comes in. We need microbes to change them. Without these relationships, the nutrients would not be available to the plant. Like plants, we form relationships with the microbes inside our Guts. They help us produce necessary nutrients like short-chain fatty acids, folate, superoxide dismutase (an enzyme antioxidant) and vitamin K and in exchange, we provide the internal garden that they grow in.

When we eat processed or refined foods, we frequently receive large amounts of empty calories or simple sugars without necessary minerals, fibers and phytonutrients. Along with the empty calories, many of these foods contain extra toxins that our bodies must throw out to maintain a clean internal environment. A build-up of the chemicals used to preserve, flavor, or enhance our foods can overload our livers. Our livers function as our filters and processing plants. They separate and distribute all the things that are absorbed into our lymph and blood streams. It is our livers' job to remove all the toxins that enter our bodies through eating, drinking, breathing or any other contact.

Often, we gulp down the fastest food available with no mind to if it is what our bodies want or need. Lack of chewing puts added pressure on the other parts of our digestive systems further down the tract. When food isn't broken down small enough and not enough saliva is added to degrade the carbohydrates, our other organs must work harder and send more enzymes. If we don't chew our food, the stomach and small intestines can't break down the food to make it ready to be absorbed. The pancreas has to help with its enzymes, but digestion takes longer and is less efficient. If this happens often, especially under stress, the food sits in our digestive systems. This invites unfriendly microorganisms to grow and create wastes inside our Guts, causing their waste products (yes, their excrements) to build up. Now, our livers are under pressure to detoxify the additional toxic wastes made by unfriendly microbes along with all of the environmental toxins that bombard us today. Our Guts and livers slow down, impacting our lymph systems. When our lymph gets backed up, we end up with hemorrhoids, varicose veins, and other problems. A sluggish liver can even reduce our metabolism making it harder to lose weight!

Eating and drinking the wrong things sludge up our livers making them inefficient, and can make us toxic and sick, but how do we know what to eat? In Genesis 1 verse 29, God said, "I give you every seed-bearing plant, which is on the face of the earth, and every tree, which has fruit yielding seed, to you it shall be for meat". Eating the right foods, in their natural state, is the way to receive the most benefit from them. I am simply talking about picking real foods and not food products. Pick foods that you can recognize, one product at a time, whole fruits, whole vegetables, and nuts, even meats (if you eat meat) that you can recognize. What are the ingredients of the food products that you eat? Do you know? Do they contain sugars, MSG or monosodium glutamate, processed fats, or other unwanted additives, clays and chemicals that clog up our inners? Are all of the nutrients processed out and a few known vitamins and minerals put back in so that they can be advertised as being healthy? Remember, if you can't recognize what the food product is, it is probably so processed that its important phytochemicals and nutrients are lost. Simply use your eyes to identify food from food-ish products.

Remember how your mother nagged you to eat your vegetables? Plants provide us with phytochemicals. Photochemicals is the general name for interactive molecules found inside plants. Some phytochemicals actively assist us in maintaining our health. They can help us stop free radical injury and control our epigenetic mechanisms. We have all heard of antioxidants, which are phytochemicals. Antioxidant is another general term used to herd up a bunch of phytochemicals that stop out-of-control molecules, called free radicals, from hurting our cells. Free radicals have lost their outer electrons and are electro magnetically unbalanced. They can cause a lot of damage while trying to replace their electrons. Antioxidants stop them. Antioxidants are only one type of the thousands of phytochemicals scientists have found so far and they have only begun to uncover them. Phytonutrients not only help us stay healthy, they can turn our DNA on and off to bring us back to health. Phytochemicals can cause the loosening of DNA coils to enable the copying of silenced genes, which are needed to recover from depression, pain, and even cancers.

We receive amino acids, carbohydrates, fatty acids, vitamins, minerals and phytonutrients from plants. Amino acids are the building blocks that we manufacture all of our bodies' chemical reactions from. They give structure to our cells, tissues and organs. Vitamins and minerals are fuel additives or cofactors that add a boost to the reactions, speeding them up and making them run. Fatty acids help us to build our cell walls and some of our hormones. Plants also give us the fiber that helps to build the compost for our internal gardens, which nurtures our friendly Gut microbial communities.

Nurturing the friendly microorganisms in our intestinal tract is more important than you think. Our Gut microbes help us absorb nutrients by making otherwise insoluble fiber available. They help us to get rid of toxins by modulating absorption and transit time. Our intestinal bacteria metabolize insoluble fiber into short-chain fatty acids, which helps to produce the energy that our colon cells use to reproduce and heal. This energy guards colon cells from cancer. Without happy Gut microbes, we are starving the cells of our colon walls. It is essential to give a garden of fiber to our microbial communities so they can provide our bodies' short-chained fatty acids, folate and vitamin K, and other factors that we need from them. Without a healthy garden, our Guts send signals of unhappiness, anxiety and lack to our brains.

We truly are dust or clay! We are the soil for approximately 100 trillion microbes. From our mouth to our rectum, we are open to the environment any time we eat, drink or even just breath. Just like our external skin, our inner membrane is covered in microbes that colonize us, work to help us receive our nutrients, help us get rid of toxins, and protect us from pathogens that can make us sick. Our healthy microbial communities prevent colonization by hostile pathogens by producing anti-microbial compounds and competing for nutrients and receptors.

The amounts and the kinds of microorganisms growing in our Guts are critical to the overall health of our temples. Common probiotic supplements, yogurts and kefirs, and fermented foods like sauerkraut contain Lactobacilli and Bifidobacterium. Adding them to our diets boost their numbers in our internal gardens. These bacteria help us fight against infections such as Listeria. Eating contaminated food causes listeriosis. Though it usually only affects older adults, newborns and people with weak immunity, for several years in a row, the Center for Disease Control and Prevention has issued multi-state warnings against listeria-tainted foods. This indicates that there is more of a danger of contracting listeria than is generally known. If we have a healthy Gut garden, our microbes are better able to fight against invaders that cause infections.

Our Gut microorganisms symbiotically take care their homes (us). We need to take care of our home in the same way. If our environment, our earth garden, becomes sick or toxic, we will become sick and die. In much the same way, because we are our microbes' gardens, if we become sick or toxic, our flora will die. It makes sense that they take care of us and that we take care of our external environment.

The microbial communities in our Guts can make us depressed or anxious or keep us happy and healthy depending on how we take care of them. Friendly Gut microbes help us cope with stress, lowers anxiety and depression. They help keep our brains plastic (changeable), learning and remembering. Our intestinal communities help us to cope with stress by lowering the release of corticosterone and adrenocorticotropin stress hormones. A lack of a healthy microbes decrease brain-derived-neurotropic-factor, which in turn, lowers the growth and survival of new neurons. This lack of healthy flora also lowers the expression or copying of the genes that make a portion of our N-Methyl-D-Aspartate (NMDA) receptors in our hippocampus and cortex. Too few NMDA receptors impair our ability to strengthen and weaken synaptic activity to improve our memory and learning functions. This means that growing the right kinds of microbes in our Guts guard our brains from aging and enhance memory and learning. They can raise our intelligence!

Some of the friendly Gut microbes colonizing our intestines modulate our anxiety and depression. Disturbing the natural balance of microbes with antibiotics can lead to colonization by pathogenic microbes. This colonization can lead to anxiety and stress-induced memory dysfunction because our memory machinery gets stuck. Eating yogurt, kefir, fermented foods or taking probiotics daily can prevent this dysfunction. Lactobacillus, a common probiotic bacterium, lowers pain and can increase the expression of receptors for natural opioids and cannabinoids in our intestinal epithelial cells. Natural opioids are known as endorphins and mimic the effects of morphine. Our little garden bugs are amazing!

Some bacteria induce increases in levels of tryptophan in our blood. The body uses tryptophan to make serotonin and melatonin. Serotonin is the key neurotransmitter in our brain/Gut/microbe axis affecting our moods and blood pressure. Melatonin helps us sleep. Tryptophan competes with other amino acids for its transport into our blood so just eating lots of turkey doesn't really help. Although, meats are high in tryptophan, they are also high in other proteins that compete for transport into the blood. These other proteins block the movement of tryptophan into the blood, which can stop the production of serotonin. Vegetable proteins don't seem to cause the same blockages.

Early life stressors have long-term affects on the composition of our Gut microbial communities. These stressors affect our immunity, anxiety and stress response leading to lower levels of Lactobacilli and Bifidobacteria. Daily separation from our main caretakers is enough stress to change our Gut microbial communities, one can only guess what chronic abuse or war could do to the balance of intestinal microbes. Our microbial composition tends to return to the balance or equilibrium founded in our first years. This is one explanation for why some of us have a more difficult time staying healthy, happy and stress free. One way to guard our infants from Gut microbial community problems is to breast-feed. Breast-feeding in a calm environment helps to initiate a healthy Gut garden and stabilize the infant's microbial community for life. A healthy internal environment facilitates our happiness and tranquility.

Both Autism and Inflammatory Bowel Disease (IBD) show alterations in the normal Gut microorganism balances and compositions. These alterations allow the colonization of pathogenic species leading to inflammation, infections, and allergic reactions. Our Gut microbes may not be the driving force causing these problems but they are definitely linked to gaining our health back. IBD affects an estimated 10-15% of the population of Western Europe and North America. Characterized by pain and combination of diarrhea and constipation, irritable bowels often occur after bacteria have caused infectious diarrhea and gastrointestinal inflammation. Post infection bowel irritability is linked to unbalanced and abnormal Gut microbes, inflammation and increased permeability of the Gut barrier.

Our Gut microorganisms communicate through the lining or epithelial cells, certain receptors, and directly with our enterochromaffin cells when our Gut lining is permeable. Enterochromaffin cells are like switchboard operators sending phone calls up to the brain and down to the Gut microbes. This may be why our Gut reactions get through to our brain with our emotions. We feel 'kicked in the Gut' or 'like crap'. The cells also send messages about pain, transport of feces and immune responses. A disruption of this communication can lead to IBD, and other acute and chronic disorders.

Diet and lifestyle control the health of our Gut microbial communities. Fatty foods can trigger symptoms as well as milk and dairy products, fried foods, spices, oranges, pastries and other sweets, pickles, onions and carbonated drinks. These and other processed foods cause the environment of our Guts to become hospitable to microbes that aren't always friendly to our health. Add chronic stress to wrong food choices and our Gut communities can be devastated. Additionally, just being over-weight can throw our Gut microbial balance off.

Taking probiotics, such as Lactobacilis helveticus and Bifidobacterium longum, normalizes immune responses. They can normalize the hyper anxiety and stress responses found in those that have suffered from early life stresses, which cause brain/Gut/microbe dysfunction. Other Lactobacilis species reduced pain normally felt with irritable bowels, as well as enhancing Gut barrier function. This can decrease a leaky Gut. Regular ingesting of Bifidobacterium normalizes irregular community ratios and enhances elimination. A multi-species probiotics treatment, taken over a 5-month period, can decrease distension and abdominal pain, and stabilize the Gut microbial community without any negative side effects.

Our Gut microorganisms can help us to fight cancer. Firmicutes, a bacterium in our Guts is a colon cancer fighter. Firmicutes use methane and undigested dietary fiber to manufacture short-chain fatty acids to maintain the health of our colon. Butyrate, one of these fatty acids, provides energy to maintain the regeneration and health of the cell walls. The energy from Butyrates regulates cell growth and differentiation. They epigenetically mediate inflammation and pain in the colon. Without Butyrates, colon cells lack energy and die. Increases in Butyrate and other short-chained fatty acids are known to epigenetically decrease our chances of cancer by stopping the removal of acetyl groups from histones that our DNA is wrapped around. Eating a diet rich in fiber and starches, which are resistant to digestion, helps to encourage the growth of these bacteria.

Colon cancer is a leading cause of cancer-related deaths in the westernized world. This may be due to the western diet of processed fast foods high in fats and sugars and low in fiber and nutrients. Without fiber, our microbes can't thrive and produce the products we need to maintain Gut health. Eating lots of vegetables and fruits that contain both soluble and insoluble fiber, and eating less meats and fats, guard and nurture our Gut microbial communities.

Our Gut is their garden! If you eat the western fast food diet, high in meats and fats, your Gut microbes produce sulfur. This sulfur alters the Gut environment and invites less friendly sulfur-eating bacteria to proliferate, which produce even more toxins. We can change our Guts from gardens to sulfur-rich hellish environments where nasty little microbes that make us ill thrive. It's our choice, the garden or hell inside our temples.

What is known so far about the microbes inside of us is only just the beginning. Scientists have found over 800 bacterial species and over 7000 different strains in our Guts. Our Guts are gardens where tiny bacteria live, grow and provide products, which interact to help our bodies and minds maintain health. They can stop depression, anxiety and even tumor growth. But, if their environment is wrong, they can degrade our moods, lower our immunities, cause inflammation and pain, and even poison our systems with their toxic waste products. Diets high in meat, fats and dairy push the friendly bacteria that are needed to maintain health out of the garden. Without our friendly microbes and the fiber they need, we can't convert fats into the useful by-products that enhance our health.

We don't know all of the microbial species needed to become a perfectly healthy temple, but we can eat in such a way as to give the correct bacteria an environment to enhance their growth. Eating a large amount of both soluble and insoluble fibers is one way to maintain a healthy intestinal environment. Fiber gives our microbes the correct environment, nutrients and helps them to transport toxins out. Giving up caffeine, alcohol, smoking, sugar, and processed foods goes a long way to nudge our gardens back to health.

When our epigenetic mechanisms are given the right tools, they can correct unwanted gene changes and protect us from mutations that could be harmful. By eating the correct plants and phytonutrients, we can control the epigenetic machinery, which can guard us from harmful mutations. For instance, a deficiency of a B vitamin found in beans, called folate, is linked to the inability of our epigenetic mechanism to add methyl groups to our DNA, especially in unborn fetuses. Because epigenetic mechanisms control how each cell is differentiated and what genes are turned on or off, this inability can cause birth defects and possibly recessive or hidden genetic defects that can be passed to our children and to their children. If folate is received, even after birth, the methyl groups can be added and the defect corrected.

Pharmaceutical companies are fabricating compounds that are ordinarily produced in our healthy Guts. One such microbial product is the short-chained fatty acid, Butyric acid. It is only produced in a healthy colon with lots of fiber in the environment. Without fiber and healthy microbes it is not produced in our colons. It is the fuel our colons cells use to reproduce. Butyric acid is important in preventing and reversing cancers and memory problems, such as those found in posttraumatic stress disorder. Unfortunately, pesticides, plants that carry pesticide genes, and a lack of natural fiber affect the health of our Gut microbial communities. Eating natural fruits and vegetables, free of pesticides and altered genomes, ensures a healthy Gut and keeps us emotionally and physically healthy without the need for pharmaceutical medications.

Butyric acid and other products are referred to as histone deacetylase inhibitors (HDACi) can be used to change how our genes are copied. Plants provide us with the same HDACi or enzymes that pharmaceutical companies are formulating and marketing. These inhibitors stop the removal of acetyl groups from our histones, which changes the coiling of our DNA. The HDACi can start a chain reaction that enables other enzymes to remove methyl groups from a silenced DNA to activate a gene. The gene can then be copied to make the proteins needed. Why is this important? Adults can benefit from HDACi treatments as well as children. In some cases, it is never to late to change our epigenetics and repair the way our genes are copied to restore and maintain our health. We can do these things using the food and medicines given to us in Genesis.

One natural source of HDACi is valerian root, an herb known for ages to enhance mood, and decrease stress, depression, and anxiety. For years, scientists thought that the components of this root were inert. Now it is thought that valproic acid, a component of valerian root, can reactivate the genes that are needed to stay emotionally balanced and even inhibit convulsions. Valerian root helps to change the gene regulation of people that have suffered sustained neglect and abuse as young children and infants. A treatment of two weeks or longer can lead to a better ability to cope with stress, anxiety, depression, and suicidal thoughts. Other natural sources of enzymes that modulate acetyl groups include hops; yes, the same stuff that is found in beer. And, no you can't drink enough beer to gain the enzyme affect. You can, however eat the herb.

Pharmaceutical companies add valproic acid to their anti-depressants and anti-anxiety medications. They use the isolated component not because it works better than the root itself, but because they can patent it. In fact, studies have shown that many whole plants work better than the isolated components, and in most cases, have less side affects. Much the same way that sugar is extracted and purified from sugar cane or beets, labs process out what they see as unnecessary junk and leave a substance that not only inhibits the removal of acetyl groups from our histones, but also is known to cause side effects. Some of the possible side effects are serious, like inflammation of the liver, renal impairment, and parkinsonian symptoms in the person taking valproic acid. While some effects are less serious like weight gain and fatigue, and some are devastating such as birth defects if taken while pregnant.

We now know that processing foods take away many phytochemicals that our bodies need. Doesn't it make sense that processing herbs for single substances probably isn't the best thing to do for the health of the patient? Scientists know that by putting together more than one HDAC inhibitor, they can reduce side effects, dosages and increase efficacy. So why take things away just to make it necessary to add things back together? Well, labs might say that the processing is needed to make the drug strong enough to work well, but if that is true, why does valerian root have such a long history of use for emotional distress? One reason may be that labs can't patent plants or whole herbs but they can patent single constituents of those herbs and market them for a number of years at a very high cost to patients. My question to you is this; why not take the whole herb? It will take longer to work because it isn't as strong but there far are fewer side effects and any side effects that may occur are mild in comparison to the isolated drug.

In Ezekiel 47 verse 12, we are told fruit trees of all kinds will grow and their fruit will be used as food and medicine. Genesis told us that all seeded fruits from trees and grain are to be used. It is reasonable to expect many different plants to interact and enhance the way they protect and aid our epigenetic mechanisms. For instance, the HDAC inhibitor found in Butyric acid is also found in many different wild parsnips and in kombucha tea, but mostly, it is a fermentation product from microbes living in our Guts. Butyric acid, as well as valproic acid can be used to aid in correcting posttraumatic stress, depression and anxiety.

Additionally, it was found that monocot plants such as the common grains of corn, rye, buckwheat and wheat can be used to generate cyclic hydroxyamic acids if their roots are harvested very young. Not only do they aid in healing depression, they also show anti-tumor activity and can help radiation kill cancer cells by making them more sensitive. Cyclic hydroxamic acid is present at high concentrations immediately after germination in wheat. Have you ever taken sprouted wheat grass juice? It is a great supplier of this HDAC inhibitor to restore and maintain emotional and physical health. You can combine many natural foods and herbs to enhance and increase the efficacy of the inhibitors and other phytochemicals that you need.

Heirloom seeds are seeds that haven't been manipulated to increase their growing behaviors. Most heirloom species of our vegetables and fruits contain increased levels of the phytochemicals that we need to maintain and return to a healthy epigenetic state in our bodies. And, since pesticides are known to cause the methylation (the hanging of methyl groups on our DNA) and silencing of important genes such as our tumor necrosis factor, it may be important to either grow your own small kitchen garden or to buy organic.

Not only do heirloom species contain more nutrients, but an article found in the Journal of Food and Chemical Toxicology showed that pesticides and genetically modified foods (GM) disrupt the endocrine system leading to breast and pituitary tumors, and liver and kidney disease. The American Cancer Society states that increased multiple myeloma or bone marrow cancer incidents are found in farm workers. Pesticides interfere with the liver's busiest pathway, the cytochrome P450 detoxification pathway and decrease our livers' abilities to synthesize hormones and clean up toxins.

Pesticides can harm the microbial communities in the soil and cause micronutrient deficiencies in plants. If pesticides can do this to the microorganisms in the soil and to plants, imagine what havoc pesticides can cause to our friendly Gut microorganisms. Our friendly Gut communities help us maintain our moods, nutrients and remain cancer free. Eating non-GM and pesticide free foods is critical to maintaining our health.

Remember, we are a part of an electromagnetic world of photons, electrons, forces and signatures. Each of us has our own frequency signature and so does everything else. In this way, everything around us affects us, and we affect everything around us. Our environment can change us, even down to our genes. Biophysicists tell us that our immune systems are highly sensitive electromagnetic sensors and the signatures of GMs are alien to our immune systems.

Scientists are now studying the affect of nutrition on our epigenetic mechanisms. The difficulty is that the nutrients interact with each other, environmental conditions like toxins, and internal components such as enzymes, hormones, and such. Stress is one of the big interacters. The hormones from stress are known to affect us epigenetically. Because researchers almost always receive their funding from corporations, corporations dictate what is studied. Promising isolated components of a plant are studied instead of the whole plant. This can lead to patents for them and side effects for us. Eating a diverse diet of natural vegetables and fruits is our best insurance.

We have only known about the ability of our genome to adapt epigenetically for a couple of decades. Scientists believed that the parts of the genome that didn't code for peptides were useless and, in fact they called them 'junk'. We now know that this 'junk' is an important part of the epigenetic mechanisms. Similarly, we call a plant a 'weed' when we don't know its medicinal and nutritional value. Scientists extract vitamins, minerals and other phytochemicals, throw the rest of the plant away, and tell us that the little pills are what we need to stay healthy. The truth is we don't need pills to stay healthy. We need a diversity of fresh whole foods that are grown in healthy, rich soils. We need foods free of pesticides, herbicides, hormones, deflocculates, and modified DNA from other things not originally found in the plants.

Corporations have benefited by patenting single constituents from plants. Many of us are taking vitamins, minerals, antioxidants, and antidepressants. Today, we know that plants contain many substances that aid in our health. We don't yet know all of them, but the Bible instructs us to eat the fruits and nuts of the trees and the field for our health and food. Processing and enriching our foods actually remove phytochemicals and fiber that may epigenetically enhance our mental, emotional and physical states. Eating whole foods, as close to their natural state as healthy, is the best way to enjoy the best health benefits. Just like the 'junk' DNA, weeds are only plants who's benefits we don't yet know. Whole plants offer many constituents that help us. Fiber, vitamins, and antioxidants are just the ones we are most familiar with. God gave us the plants and herbs to use. Don't let marketing, packaging, and ease of use, rob you of the positive affects of real whole foods.

The study of the epigenetics of foods and herbs is in its infancy and we still don't know all about which plants are best to use for what. What we do know is that the nutrients found in plants can reverse or change epigenetic phenomena and modify the expression or copying of critical genes. These critical genes are associated with embryonic development, aging, and cancer growth. The correct nutrients can prevent the problems in genes associated with autoimmunity problems like rheumatoid arthritis. Some examples of plants that modulate our epigenetic mechanisms include: green tea, broccoli, garlic, fiber, valerian, grapes, and hops. This list names only a few that are being studied. Thankfully, we don't need to know them all to improve our health. In the Bible, we are told that *every* herb is given to us for our use. Eating a diversity of fruits and vegetables helps to ensure our health. Using the whole food and not just the isolated nutrient lowers side effects and works synergistically to bolster our bodies. Simply, the whole plant usually works better than the chemical. We can negatively or positively affect our health through manipulating our epigenetic mechanisms throughout our lives. This gives us great power over our heath and well-being. The choice is ours. It always was.

Dust to Dust

The United States Department of Agriculture (USDA) says that there are between 100 million and 1 billion bacteria in a teaspoon of productive soil. There are also fungi and other microorganisms at work. Similar to inside our Guts, microbes maintain the health of the soil and the plants. Most of the soil organisms are decomposers that maintain healthy levels of nutrients such as carbon and nitrogen. They make the nutrients available to plants. They are the planets garbage collectors and processors. Without them, we would be surrounded in dead things and pollutants. Some of them even break down pesticides and toxins in the soil.

Bacteria also form partnerships with plants and animals. They also work in partnership in our Guts. These partnerships help to produce products that humans, other animals, and plants need to survive. Scientists are just beginning to understand all of the microbial interactions that take place inside the soil and inside our bodies. Not only do microorganisms aid digestion, elimination, immunity and inflammation, it is now thought that the microorganisms in our Guts can alter the way our genes are expressed. This may sound impossible but there are many examples of microorganisms changing the behavior of mammals and insects. Scientists have found that Cordycepts, a well-known fungus, can grow in the brain of an ant. Just before the fungus kills the ant and sprouts a mushroom from the head of the ant, it causes the ant to climb down from its ant colony to bite a leaf. The fungus does this in order to find the ideal environment to disperse its spores and infect other foraging ants. The fungus literally controls the ant's behavior.

This microbial-insect interaction gets even more complex. The ants herd and farm an insect called a hemipteran. Hemipterans are tiny, plant phloem or plant blood feeding insects. Ants protect and herd them for a sweet milk-like secretion that the ants drink. The hemipterans and the ants both transmit viral, bacterial, and fungal infections to the plants. Cocoa and cassava farmers in Ghana need to stop the ants and hemipterans from infecting their plants with the virus, so they use cordycepts to stop them. They are infecting ants with cordycepts in order to protect the plants from diseases. We are still not sure how the plants react to the bite of the cordycept-infected ants or if cordycepts are passed to us if we eat the plants. Interestingly, cordycepts have been used in oriental medicine, and according to WebMD, they strengthen immunity, improve liver function and promote longer life, obviously exhibiting a positive affect in humans.

Similarly, baculoviruses infect moth caterpillars and manipulate them, in order to get them to the treetops. A baculovirus, Lymantria dispar nucleopolyhedrovirus, causes climbing behavior in the European gypsy moth, in order to release infective viral particles from the best vantage point. This is how the baculovirus reproduces. Usually, healthy gypsy moths hide under leaves to avoid being eaten by predators during the day and climb out to feed after dark, but an infected one climbs to the top of the leaves during daylight. Dr. Rollie Clem, from University of Kansas, showed that if you take away a certain (egt) gene's ability to activate in the baculovirus' genome, it stopped the climbing behavior in the moths, while the moths infected with the baculovirus with intact egt genes still exhibited the climbing behavior. This proves that the genes of one organism can affect the gene expression of another organism.

Why is this important to us? You might argue that these are only examples of insects and microbes, but mammals can be manipulated as well! An example of an organism controlling a mammal's brain is a protozoan parasite called Toxoplasma gondii, which infects the brains of mice. This organism causes mice to be attracted to cats. Once the cat eats the infected mouse, the organism is free the start a new cycle of life in its new host, the cat. The latent toxoplasma infection causes a decrease in locomotion and a drop in predator avoidance behaviors in rats, which scientists believe is a lack of exploration caused by a rise in dopamine levels. Studies, from Oxford University of Veterinary Services, have shown that mice with toxoplasma gondii infections have a 114% increase in dopamine levels.

In humans, latent toxoplasma gondii infections are fairly common. The Center for Disease Control reports up to 80% of the populations of developed countries, especially among people with cats are infected. Until recently, it was thought that the only problems caused by the infection in humans were connected with its transmission during pregnancy. However, many studies publish on Pubmed now reveal that latent toxoplasma gondii infections cause subtle changes to the personality and psychomotor performance of men and women. These changes include a rise in traffic accidents among people with latent infections. Infected men are more likely to disregard rules and were more expedient, suspicious, jealous, and dogmatic. Women were affect in the opposite way and became more compliant. Both sexes were more apprehensive. These results seem consistent with the effects of toxoplasma gondii on rodents indicating that the infection affects the dopamine and possibly the testosterone levels in humans.

While we, as yet, have no direct proof in human studies that the genetic material of organisms such as bacteria control the expression of our genes, we do have proof that organisms can control the amount of neurotransmitters that occur in our brains. They can manipulate our reward processes! We also know that microorganisms can take control of the brains of other mammals. Is it such a jump to think that science will soon prove that microorganisms can affect the expression of our genes? We have more microbes in our bodies than we have cells! We have just begun to reveal the importance of the interactions that take place in our intestine.

Canadian research on mice with microbe-free intestine found changes in fat metabolism and stress behaviors. Gut microbial communities can influence the energy balance of our bodies as well as our dopamine and serotonin circuitry. The brain-Gut-enteric microbiota axis includes the central nervous system, our sympathetic and parasympathetic nervous systems, our hormone and immune systems, the enteric nervous system (the nerve system in our intestines or Guts) and the intestinal microbiota. These systems form a network that connects our brains to our Guts through nerve fibers. This system influences our motor, sensory and secretory systems. Our Guts, through our vagus nerves, can influence our brains' function. This network influences our moods, our metabolism and our immunity. Microbes influence us!

Our gastrointestinal tracts contain 10 times more microorganisms than the number of cells in our bodies and there are possibly more than one thousand different species in an adult's intestine. Dominated by mostly anaerobic bacteria (those that don't use oxygen), we also have viruses, protozoa, archae, and fungi. The balance of these organisms is what benefits our health, while changes in our flora can destabilize our equilibrium and cause disease. Altering our beneficial bacteria can negatively impact our health. Infections, diet and antibiotics alter our flora, and age also influences our intestinal microbiota. The changes found due to aging are linked to a decline in the health of the individual. This is another reason to eat correctly. Diet alters our flora. What these little creatures eat, secrete, and expel, are very important to the health of our bodies. The wrong ones can make toxins that can cause us to become very ill. Unfortunately, the typical western diet is thought to cause an alteration of microbiota strains that enhance proinflammatory responses.

Diet may be more interactive with our genomes than was once thought. Do you remember the 'junk' DNA that scientists thought didn't code for anything? We now know that these tiny bits of DNA are codes for what is called microRNA. MicroRNA grabs hold of the machinery called messenger RNA (mRNA), which helps to build amino acids and proteins. MicroRNA influences how mRNA constructs peptides and proteins. Until recently, it wasn't believed that these little snippets of DNA could affect genomes other than their own. But, in a Chinese study published in 2012 by Cell Research, the microRNA from rice was found attached to the mRNA of people that eat a diet primarily made up of rice. The attachment regulated the way the gene was expressed or copied. The rice gene altered a human gene! This really gives new meaning to the phrase 'you are what you eat'. The snippets of DNA from the rice can affect the way people use their genes to make amino acids and proteins. Knowing these things, ask yourselves if you think that it is in our best interest to eat food whose genomes have been altered to contain parts of the genome of bacterium found breaking down pesticides and containing antibiotic? We don't have enough direct proof that they negatively affect the microorganisms of our intestines or our gene expression, but how long did it take to get direct proof that cigarettes cause cancer and effect our gene expression?

Scientists add or splice antibiotic resistance genes into the genome of their genetically modified plants in order to test the plant for the gene modification that they are trying to achieve. Do we really want the possibility of antibiotic resistance jumping from one species to another? Bacteria share DNA as part of their cell division and reproduction, and microorganisms and plants share between each other too. The sharing of rice microRNA in people that have a rice-based diet is proof that plants and animals share too! We can't escape it; we share everything with the universe around us at the level of Spirit or energy and dust or matter. Bees change a normal egg into a queen, merely by feeding the infant royal jelly to change its epigenetic make up. I can't help but wonder how John the Baptist's diet of honey and locust would affect our epigenetics.

It is important to our health to consider our bodies and flora including our intestinal microbial communities as a whole, assessing all of the interactions together. A multidisciplinary approach to health is needed including psychiatry, microbiology, ecology, toxicology and neuroscience. And, if we look at the research, a spiritual approach is also needed. Praise, prayer and meditation are crucial tools in maintaining our body temples.

The Bible tells us that God formed us from the clay and then breathed spirit into us. We are energy and matter. We are Spirit and dust. Physicists believe that the dust that we are made of consists of stardust. The dust from exploding stars gathered to form the earth in a process called accretion. The part of us that is dust contains not only of the soil of the earth, but also the interactions of the creatures found in the soil, which are recycled and reused. A delicate exchange of energy insures the existence of this environment with microorganisms forming the bases of the energy reprocessing.

It is no surprise that electromagnetic radiation, even at extremely low levels, affects everything on earth when we realize that we are merely interactions of energy fields moving around in infinite energy. Olle Johansson, a neuroscientist from Stockholm, Sweden warns in a review titled, Disturbance of the immune system by electromagnetic fields, that the man-made electromagnetic fields cause disturbances in our ability to correct and repair our cells. This increases risks for cancer, and neurological and DNA damage at levels much lower than safety standards require. Johansson warns, "Very often the biggest threat from EMF exposure is said to be cancer. However, this is not the most horrifying scenario…Imagine if one morning the nitrogen-binding bacteria in the soil or the honeybees in the air had been destroyed beyond repair…if our immune system, trying to cope with the ever-increasing electromagnetic signals, finally could not do so any longer!" We cannot manipulate energy fields without consequences, and we must understand and acknowledge the possible interactions. We are intimately connected to the environment around us. It affects our health and happiness. Like the different bands of light in a rainbow, we are the infinite energy field dividing to make-up individual colors or personalities that actually belong to the whole. We are light! We are Spirit energy. Everything is energy. A pulse of electricity can end a life or start a heart depending on the hand holding the energy. Let's use it responsibly.

Do you remember the invisibility cloak I mentioned in the introduction chapter? Duke University's Pratt School of Engineering demonstrated, in October of 2006, that we could become invisible to microwaves using copper mesh and conducting epoxy. These metamaterials deflect the microwaves so that they flow around the cloak. Today, we can protect ourselves from the microwaves of our cell phones and towers using these technologies, but how will we protect the bees, microbes and other creatures that share our environment?

We are taught that the food web or chain includes plants and animals, with ourselves at the top. Sometimes, worms, bees and other things are included, but science tells us that the interactions that share energy are much more complicated. Plants gain their fuel from the energy of light and use it to build their physical bodies. But, is that all there is to the complexity of the food chain? While hiking, I climbed up a jumble of boulders to the top, where I sat quietly watching the birds and the bugs flying in the sunlight. I noticed a large beetle harvesting the green lichen. Knowing that the lichen was feasting on the boulder, it made me wonder where the food chain or web really starts. The earth folds and swallows the land and the continents down, churning and spiting new material out in the forms of crystals, glass, all forms of rock, water and oxygen. The lichen consumes this material in the form of boulders. Its leftovers are called reolith, the new baby soil of the earth. And, the beetle eats the lichen; the bird eats the beetle, and so on.

Why do we assume the food web begins with plants when plants need the soil that is spit up from the earth, broken down by lichen or recycled by the microbes? Why do we assume there is no life beyond our carbon-based paradigm? Scientists measure the photons emitting from a test tube before they measure the substance and the tube together. They do this because the tubes emit small amounts of photons of their own too. Every stone emits photon energy. In Luke chapter 19, Jesus told us that if the disciples didn't announce his coming and who he was, the stones would cry out. In Habakkuk 2 verse 11, we are told that the stones of the wall and the wood of the ceiling beams answer each other. Stones can bare witness against us and the stones of Jericho fell on our command. Why do we assume that life stops with things that move and breathe like us when everything is made of Divine Energy?

The major elemental building blocks of our bodies consist of: carbon, oxygen, hydrogen, nitrogen and sulfur. These are the very same elements that we find all around us. Our bodies are made up of more than 70% water and the rest are merely trace metals or salts, gases and a bit of carbon. The very same things the animals are constructed from. God gave Adam stewardship over the animals. We named the animals like we name our children and were given rule over them. In Ecclesiastes 3, verse 21 King Solomon asked, "Who knows if the spirit of man rises upward and if the spirit of the animal goes down into the earth?" If King Solomon didn't know if animals had spirits, how can we rationalize mistreatment of them? Respecting the quality of life of our animals is imperative to our own quality of life. As we have seen, keeping our external and internal environments pristine ensures the health of everything that shares our Earth.

Light is the power that fuels the earth. Through photosynthesis, plants gather the energy of the photons, and the minerals and water from the earth. They too are Spirit and dust. Plants change this energy into carbohydrates that feed humans, animals, insects, and microbes. We even share the building block for copying our genetic codes with them. The microbes transform the minerals into easily assimilated pieces and recycle the leftovers. Everything material returns to dust, either directly, or by way of another creature consuming energy and transforming it yet again.

We share the infinite energy source with everything. Hawking tells us that all matter in this universe came from an infinitely dense, infinitely small singularity. What this means is we were once all unified and entangled. What is entangled? Entangled is how particles, that were once joined and then separated, still act as if they are together. If the rotation of one of the particles is changed, the rotation of the other is changed even if it is eighty miles away. Stanford University sends information this way instantly. They call it teleportation! The Nippon Telegraph and Telephone Corporation of Japan is using teleportation to speed communications to faster than the speed of light. This works because the particles are unified. What happens to one happens to the other. We are unified! What happens to one happens to all.

The Spirit in each one of us shares infinite energy and information with the rest of the universe. When that energy is removed, the dust continues the cycle of decomposition back to nutrients and energy. The Bible promises us one hundred and twenty years before the Spirit is taken back. It also tells us how to maintain a healthy and joyful state throughout. Completely accepting that we are eternal Spirit transforms our mental, emotional and physical states. Believing, no, knowing that we are the temples that house infinite Spirit is as easy as measuring the firing of our neurons on an EEG machine. The measured brainwaves are created and maintained by the electrons and photons that spring from the electromagnetic energy field of our universe.

An infinite, electromagnetic field produces the electrons and photons that power our bodies. Energy waves react with our senses to inform us about the universe. The firing of our mirror neurons tells us that our brothers are ourselves. Music synchronizes the frequencies of our brainwaves and allows us to send energy out into the universe in praise and song as a unit. The emotions of love fire neurons that send hormones to our brains telling us that we are one with another person. Our cells recognize the odor of another and tell us to love them as our same body. Loving God, the infinite energy source, ultimately means loving ourselves. But then, our commandments were to love God and to love our neighbors as ourselves.

How we choose to think guides how energy is routed inside of our nervous system. Energy can switch on fight and flight or rest and restore, it is all controlled by how we choose to think about the universe around us. We are told in Colossians 3, verses 12-16, "put on a heart of compassion, kindness, humility, gentleness and patience, bearing with one another, and forgiving each other, whoever has a complaint against anyone; just as the Lord forgave you, so also should you. Beyond all these things put on love, which is the perfect bond of unity. Let the peace of Christ rule in your hearts, to which indeed you were called in one body; and be thankful. Let the message of Christ dwell among you richly as you teach and admonish one another with all wisdom through psalms, hymns, and songs from the Spirit, singing to God with gratitude in your hearts."

Lets review! This passage instructed us to have compassion, kindness, and humility, to put up with and forgive each other, to love each other as one, to have peace through the belief that we truly are one, and to be grateful. I don't think the instructions for health and happiness could have been said better! This is a recipe for the care of our bodies, the Temples of the Holy Spirit.

Every organism, tissue, cell or protein can be explained in two ways. The biochemical explanation is the one we all learned in school using molecules and thinking of ourselves as solid. The bioelectromagnetic approach tells us that we are negative and positive forces pulling together and pushing apart with the energy of the electrons and protons. Jeffery Driban, a researcher from Tufts University, stated very succinctly in an article detailing the electrical changes after surgery, "Every physiologic event can be defined by mutually dependent biochemical and bioelectromagnetic characteristics. For example, when a muscle contracts, the cells generate electric potentials due to the flow of ions across the cell membranes." We are comfortable with the chemical building-block explanation of our bodies because it is familiar, but it is no more accurate than believing the earth is flat. We are beings constructed of the interactions of infinite energy!

Infinite energy interacts with and through our bodies. Our cells use this external energy to sense our environments and to direct their functions. We control how this energy is used with our beliefs and perceptions. We have the power to control our health. We can control how our DNA is used! If you are ill, you are not stuck; the Bible gives us the instructions to transform our bodies and our minds. Gratitude, trust, faith, forgiveness, compassion, prayer, meditation, praise, fasting, and properly eating God's given foods are all tools we can use to gain and maintain physical, mental and emotional vitality, and well-being. You can to choose to use the knowledge! The infinite Spirit abides in you. You are a **Temple**.

Made in the USA
Columbia, SC
05 March 2018